THE HISTORY OF TAXATION IN NORTH CAROLINA DURING THE COLONIAL PERIOD

1663-1776

BY

CORALIE PARKER

SUBMITTED IN PARTIAL FULFILLMENT OF THE REQUIREMENTS
FOR THE DEGREE OF DOCTOR OF PHILOSOPHY
IN THE FACULTY OF POLITICAL SCIENCE
COLUMBIA UNIVERSITY

Southern Historical Press, Inc.
Greenville, South Carolina

SOUTHERN HISTORICAL PRESS, INC.
PO BOX 1267
Greenville, SC   29601

ISBN #978-1-63914-085-5

Printed in the United States of America

To My
MOTHER AND FATHER
GRATITUDE AND RESPECT

PREFACE

WITH the increasing complexity of economic conditions in modern society, a vigorous interest in fiscal problems becomes widespread, especially in the domain of taxation. The complicated field of taxation in the United States presents a multiplicity of questions for examination, the solution of which often becomes problematical. It is probable that the key to many of these problems may be found in a study of the origin of these taxes. For this reason, a study of the various systems of financing employed by the different colonies from which the states developed may prove beneficial to students of taxation.

The object of this study is to present a description of the fiscal conditions accompanying the formation of one link in the chain of states, with their different methods of financing, out of which grew the present taxation system in the United States. Explanation and discussion are offered of the revenues in the colony of North Carolina from the time it came into the possession of the Lords Proprietors in 1663, and afterwards when it was purchased by the English Crown in 1729, until the Declaration of Independence in 1776. The introductory chapter contains a succinct description of the prevailing economic philosophy of that time, with a brief account of the English system of taxation, which was the background of the methods of taxation used in colonial North Carolina.

The materials used in this book were drawn from the records, laws and writings of the period under discussion. A careful research was made into the subject, and the facts obtained, I believe, justify the conclusions made.

I am happy to be permitted this opportunity to express my appreciation to Professor E. R. A. Seligman for the privilege of working in this particular division of study, and for the helpful suggestions and valuable criticisms which he so graciously has given me in this work, and to Professor V. G. Simkhovitch, Professor H. R. Seager, Professor R. L. Schuyler and the other members of the Faculty of Political Science of Columbia University who have contributed their time in examining this study. I am glad to acknowledge my indebtedness to Professors D. D. Carroll, R. D. W. Connor, C. P. Spruill, and M. S. Heath of the University of North Carolina for their cordial coöperation and assistance in the preparation of the material for this book. I take, also, a particular pleasure in expressing my thanks to Dr. Francis D. Winston, a trustee of the University of North Carolina, for the opportunity of engaging in this specific piece of research.

CORALIE PARKER.

Columbia University,
New York City.

CONTENTS

The History of Taxation in North Carolina during the Colonial Period, 1663-1776

CHAPTER I

INTRODUCTION

IN order to understand any phase of the economic development of the American states along the Atlantic
coast, it is necessary to examine the genesis, in English
history, of the actual formation of each particular colony.
The derivation from England of the state of North Carolina, the subject of our study, with its rudimentary
stage in Albemarle and the Cape Fear region, constitutes
one of the most picturesque episodes in all the process
of settlement of the English colonial possessions in
North America.

Although English-speaking people began coming to
North Carolina in the last quarter of the sixteenth century its permanent governmental establishment did not
materialize until the last half of the seventeenth century,
when Charles II granted this territory to eight of his
deserving subjects, afterwards known as the Lords
Proprietors. The seventeenth century marks the formation of North Carolina as an English colonial territory.
For more than a hundred years afterward, until the last
quarter of the eighteenth century, North Carolina remained a colonial possession of England. It was governed by the Lords Proprietors from its establishment
in 1663 until 1729, when the Crown bought this territory, which it held until the Declaration of Independ-

ence in 1776. To perceive the true significance of events occurring in the territory during this period, the political and economic theories and policies of England during the seventeenth and eighteenth centuries should be reviewed.

The Foundation of Mercantilism. During the three centuries following the medieval period there gradually came into existence a combination of economic ideas and governmental policies to which most historians have applied the term "mercantilism." Roughly speaking, this period may be said to cover the major part of the sixteenth, seventeenth and eighteenth centuries. The majority of these policies were confined to commerce and problems relating to commercial life with its attendant restrictions. The foundations of mercantilism were the expansion of money economy and the formation of nations.[1] One of the principal economic elements underlying mercantilism was an exchange economy. The origin and the diffusion of a money economy were characteristics of the mercantile period. Before the decline of feudalism and the manorial system, with its domestic economy, in which each manor, ruled by a lord, formed a relatively self-sufficient economic unit producing almost all of the commodities required for its consumption and needing little or no exchange, there arose the freeman of the towns with their guild system of industry.[2] This necessitated a system of exchange.

With the decline of the manorial and guild systems, the domestic system of manufacture appeared. The great woolen and worsted industries in Yorkshire and other parts of England came into existence. During the sixteenth century, England had begun to export woolen ma-

---

[1] Haney, L. H., *History of Economic Thought,* p. 104.
[2] Ashley, W. J., *English Economic History,* pp. 42–52.

terials instead of the raw commodity, wool. "Enclosures," free labor, a decline in monopolies, and a rise of competition in industry were conditions existing in the seventeenth century,[3] and internal and external commerce was augmented, resulting in increasing exchange.

As exchange was accelerated, a need for a single medium asserted itself, and from the various articles used for this purpose gold and silver coins as money were gradually selected; a money economy had evolved. The supply of bullion was increased by the discovery of new silver mines in America. In the middle of the seventeenth century money-lending and a primitive form of banking were carried on by goldsmiths,[4] and a majority of the loans were advanced by the goldsmiths to the sovereign who used taxes as a pledge of security. Some goldsmiths of London made a very large loan to Charles II, with interest to accrue at 8 to 10 per cent; this loan was secured by taxes. In 1672 this monarch refused to pay anything but the interest on the loan and closed the treasury—an act which precipitated a violent panic in the business world.[5] Near the end of the century, among other causes, a need for a more reliable manner of making loans resulted in the establishment of the Bank of England in 1694.[6]

The mining of a large quantity of bullion initiated a rise in prices which was the cause of much thought, and, influenced by the financial difficulties of the government together with the discontent of the laboring classes, many able men attempted a solution of the problems involved.[7] In England during the seventeenth century, mercantilist

[3] Gibbins, H. De B., *Industry in England*, pp. 284–317.
[4] *Ibid.*, p. 299.
[5] Cunningham, W., *Growth of Industry and Commerce*, Vol. II, p. 223.
[6] Gibbins, H. De B., *Industry in England*, p. 300.
[7] Haney, L. H., *History of Economic Thought*, p. 106.

writers were numerous and their works were prolific.[8] Court extravagances and the need of greater expenditures for promoting the welfare of the government made necessary an increase in taxation. Commerce and industry, with a growth in the supply of money, were laying an adequate foundation for taxation.[9]

The existence of a money economy and many subsequent economic changes, such as new systems of communication, a more elastic machinery of credit, the rise of the press and a geographical division of labor, together with the transition of the domestic system of industry, destined England to rise—like many other countries during the sixteenth century—to form a nation.[10] States forming economic units and conscious of their strength, combined these interests with political considerations. This development and the rise of nations formed the essence of mercantilism. Schmoller's interpretation of mercantilism is illuminating: "Only he who thus conceives of mercantilism will understand it; in its innermost kernel it is nothing but state making—not state making in a narrow sense, but state making and national-economy making at the same time; state making in the modern sense, which creates out of the political community an economic community, and so gives it a heightened meaning. The essence of the system lies . . . in the total transformation of society and its organization, as well as of the state and its institutions, in the replacing of a local and territorial economic policy by that of the national

---

[8] Hobbes, Harrison, Thomas Munn, John Locke, Sir Josiah Child, Robert Clanell, Sir William Petty and Sir Dudley North were among the prominent ones.

[9] Haney, L. H., *History of Economic Thought*, p. 106.

[10] Schmoller, G., *The Mercantile System and Its Historical Significance*, pp. 46-47.

state. . . ." [11] Each state was grasping for power, an effort which was reflected in many ways, such as high duties in one place and low duties in another. The general idea prevalent during the seventeenth and eighteenth centuries was "to cast the weight of the power of the state into the scales of the balance in the way demanded in each case by national interests" [12] as competitions veered, throwing power from one nation to another.

The Theory and Policy of Mercantilism. In discussion of the theories and policies of mercantilism, one purpose seems to have predominated: namely, to make the state strong. Wealth, being the economic basis for strength, was given an important place, and the precious metals were considered the most important form of wealth. Foreign trade was generally held in higher esteem than any other form of enterprise, for through this means the precious metals could best be obtained. In judging the success of this policy, much consideration was given to the idea of the balance of trade.[13] Mercantilism seems to have had the same relation to trade as feudalism had to land; in a way, mercantilism was the successor of feudalism.

During the seventeenth century England was just acquiring her place of dominance among the European countries. This was also a period of financial strain for her; the rise of prices made government more expensive to maintain. Since the Puritans were deplorable financiers, under their régime England became bankrupt, and it was not until 1689 that her finances were placed on a sound basis.

[11] Schmoller, G., *The Mercantile System and Its Historical Significance,* pp. 50–51.

[12] *Ibid.*, p. 59.

[13] Haney, L. H., *History of Economic Thought,* p. 109.

By the middle of the seventeenth century England was isolated, for she had lost Calais in 1557 and was thus excluded from possession of territory on the Continent. At this time she was undeveloped and her population during the seventeenth century was from four to five million; in the eighteenth century there were from five to eight million. The discovery of new trade routes to America and India offered her innumerable riches; ships, trade and navigation followed as a result, until, by the end of the seventeenth century, commerce had become an element of paramount importance in England's political and economic life. The English people began to wish for national strength. They desired their country to be prosperous, to obtain leadership among other nations, and to be powerful as a nation. The prevailing philosophy tended to exalt the welfare of the state regardless of the individual, or of groups of individuals, such as the colonies. This, the mercantile philosophy, is the principle which usually controls in any newly formed state.

During the seventeenth and eighteenth centuries there was continuous antagonism between land and trade. Parliament, which was controlled by the landowners, dared not favor the merchants unless the landowners assented, an attitude which was reflected in the struggle between customs duties and land taxes throughout this period. The landowners in general favored duties placed on commerce, with fewer taxes on land, for defraying the expenses of government. The importers and exporters protested against this imposition; trade, however, was rapidly becoming an important factor in the production of national wealth and while manufacturing was not at the time important, it was governed by the merchants in a manner which was one of the peculiarities of the system of industry prevalent in England during this period. In spite of the important rôle of mercantilism, agriculture retained its supremacy during the seventeenth and eighteenth centuries.

During this period trade flourished, for the great interest taken in the so-called balance of trade was one of the characteristics of mercantilism. There were two factors involved in the idea of trade: the general balance, which received chief attention, and the individual balance of each country. The colonies were confronted with the same problem which England had to face. Trade was thought to be the principal source of wealth; wealth, the source of power. Since the promotion of trade was incumbent upon the state, this period presented a complexity of treaties between all of the various nations, each one attempting to effect satisfactory conditions for itself. On every hand the slogans, "balance of trade" and "balance of power" were sounded. The conflict between nations during the mercantile period was based upon the misleading concept that what one nation gained, another lost. The concept of a generally increasing wealth, where benefit to one nation resulted in benefit to all, had not then come into existence. The idea that the purpose of the mercantilist, especially in England after the seventeenth century, was to acquire as much gold and silver as possible, should not be taken too literally. The mercantilist welcomed everything which would promote the wealth and power of the country; bullion, credits, and bank notes were as acceptable as gold and silver coins. It was money for use as a reserve credit power within the country which was desired in place of consumers' and producers' commodities.

The Colonial Policy of England. England's fear of the Dutch prior to 1650 was the cause of the development of great trade rivalry among the nations, a rivalry which was to last until about 1689. Holland had, however, been reduced to a secondary rank among commercial nations when the rivalry between England and France began.[14] In 1678, by an act of the British Parliament, the importation of French goods was prohibited, a step which placed England in such a position of isolation that she was practically compelled to develop trade with her colonies.

Not until the last decade of the seventeenth century did mercantilism in England attain its real significance, with the development of the theory of an empire forming an economic unit complete within itself. England, the mother country, was to be the center of the system; surrounding her, and next in rank, were the colonies producing sugar and tobacco, while the colonies which supplied such commodities such as breads and other food supplies ranged on the outer border. England, with this series of systematic groupings, was to be self-sufficing, carrying on her trade among all her component parts. This represented the ideal of the mercantilist.

The trend of the forces shaping English governmental policies of colonial trade during this century was toward centralization and systematization. After the Restoration of Charles II, Parliament had assumed control of commercial regulations between England and her colonies, and although Parliament had control of legislative matters concerning navigation and trade, it was the duty of the King to supervise the execution of these laws. Provinces were added to the domain of the Crown in increasing numbers until the culmination of the movement, about the middle of the eighteenth century. The annexation to the Crown of these new provinces, such as Jamaica, on the Virginia pattern, and the union of the New England

[14] Andrews, C. M., *The Colonial Period,* pp. 223–224.

colonies with New York in the dominion of New England together with the administration of the new trade and navigation laws, necessitated much more work on the part of the royal executive.[15] As colonial trade increased, many political and economic questions were presented for solution.

The Offices of Administration in England. Although the actual work was done through ministers, councils, commissioners and boards of various kinds, the determination of such questions lay, in the final analysis, with the King. The most important of the advisory bodies, and the nucleus around which all other administrative offices were grouped, was the Privy Council. This body communicated directly with the King and issued orders to the other executive branches of government, thus forming with the King a unified instrument of government.[16] Although there were various departments grouped around this central body, there was at this time no office established for the particular business of attending to colonial affairs, so these duties were imposed upon the Privy Council, which appointed a general committee charged with attending to colonial business. The task of the Privy Council was concerned chiefly with discussions and decisions, the practical application of which devolved upon one of the secretaries of state, who were the executives for the Privy Council.

In view of the rapid growth, during the seventeenth century, in trade relations and because of the colonial questions involved, the fact is self-evident that the Privy Council and its committees were inadequate for the supervision of such matters. The attention of the members of this council and these committees was occupied with internal af-

---

[15] Beer, G. L., *The Old Colonial System*, Part I, Vol. I, p. 226.
[16] *Ibid.*, p. 228.

fairs, and the colonies received consideration only after the more important adjustments at home had been made. Then, too, regardless of the amount of interest which any of these statesmen might evince towards the colonies, they were handicapped in the rendering of possible assistance by a lack of expert information. With the recognition of this fact, a need arose for a group of advisors, with expert knowledge about the colonies, to apply its time exclusively to the deliberation of colonial affairs. As a result of this demand, there was created in December, 1660, the Council for Foreign Plantations [17] composed of groups representing a variety of interests. There were men like the first Earl of Shaftesbury and other incumbents of some of the highest official posts in the kingdom; as well as Lord Berkeley, Sir George Carteret and John Colleton, who were interested in the financial returns of enterprises conducted in some of the colonies. Another member of this group was Edward Diggs of Virginia, who possessed experience in the colonies as commissioner of planters or traders. It was the duty of this Council for Foreign Plantations to inform itself concerning the general conditions in the colonies and to make reports to the King; to render these colonies useful to England, and vice versa; to establish a more symmetrical form of government; and to enforce the navigation acts.

The ideas of commerce and colonization were, at this time, inseparable. England planted colonies with a view to promoting trade for herself, which accounts for the creation, about a month before the establishment of the Council for Foreign Plantations, of a Council for Trade charged with the supervision of commercial matters. It was the duty of this Council to promote the

[17] Beer, G. L., *The Old Colonial System*, Part I, Vol. I, pp. 231–232.

welfare of the colonies and to advance their trade with England, as well as to make suggestions concerning the tariff. These two bodies, the Council for Foreign Plantations and the Council for Trade, remained in existence, however, only about four years, and expired chiefly because of lack of authority and withholding by the Privy Council of any real responsibility. After Clarendon's loss of power, there was a reorganization in 1668 of the Privy Council with several committees, the most important being the one for trade and plantations, of which Lord Ashley and Sir George Carteret were members. Later, in 1670, the colonial council was reestablished under a system which provided for a reduction in the number of members, and for the remuneration for their services, a provision which made the position of this body more commanding. During the following year, to lend influence and dignity to the commission, prominent statesmen and royalty were made honorary members.

The Council of Trade was gradually forced into this more alert special colonial council, with the result that in 1672 a new commission, known as the Council for Trade and Plantations, was created with the Earl of Shaftesbury as its president, and Dr. Benjamin Morsley, an authority on the economic conditions of the colonies, as its first secretary. It is interesting to note that Morsley's successor in 1673 was John Locke, the philosopher. During a period of four years this body was engaged in improving imperial control; it held meetings, heard complaints of various kinds, kept in close touch with conditions in the colonies, and made reports of this information to the Privy Council. It prepared and sent instructions to the governors of the colonies and kept watch over their legislative enactments in order that the imperial interests of England might not thereby be jeopardized.

When, after the fall of Shaftesbury in 1673, the Earl of Danby became Chief Minister to the King, he inaugurated a policy of economy which resulted eventually in the dissolution of the Council. In its place Charles II appointed a group of men called the Lords of Trade, who carefully inspected all economic and political questions in regard to the colonies, and instituted policies which resulted in a rigid administration of the laws of trade and navigation. There were two other "administrative departments" to assist in this work: the Treasury and the Admiralty.[18] The Treasury, with its commissioners of customs, and the Admiralty with its navy, were important factors in the enforcement of the laws of navigation and trade.[19]

The colonies often came in contact with the three branches of the English Treasury System: namely, the Treasury Board, the Exchequer, and the Bank of England. The Treasury Board regulated the financial policies of the Kingdom; the Exchequer had charge of keeping the list of receipts and expenditures; and the Bank of England held the money.[20] The commissioners of customs and other boards were likewise under the jurisdiction of the Treasury. The Treasury was concerned in gaining possession of that part of the confiscations—resulting from the violation of the Acts of Trade—which up to that time had reverted to the Crown. This department was interested in enforcing those statutes that operated to bring revenue into the Treasury, although actual administration of such laws was in the hands of England's customs officials who issued the bonds permitting ships to sail from the country.[21] The enumeration

[18] Beer, G. L., *The Old Colonial System*, Part I, Vol. I, p. 259.
[19] *Ibid.*, p. 260.
[20] Andrews, C. M., *The Colonial Period*, p. 131.
[21] Beer, G. L., *The Old Colonial System*, Part I, Vol. I, p. 261.

clauses, therefore, were under the domination of the Treasury, a power which was increased in 1673 through Parliament's placing the collection of plantation duties in the hands of the commissioners of the customs. This body appointed collectors of customs in some of the colonies with a comptroller, who was also a surveyor general, to countersign accounts which the collectors sent to England. The entire body of commercial regulations was under the final control of the Treasury, which often issued instructions directly to the governors in the colonies.[22]

The Admiralty Department in England, although in existence several years before the Restoration, was not active until James, Duke of York, became the Lord High Admiral of England.[23] He was given power over the colonies in 1662 [24] and admiralty courts were held before which cases of violation of the commercial laws were brought for trial. The Lord High Admiral appointed deputies with courts in the colonies belonging to the Crown, and trading ships evading the law were watched and seized by the navy. "The Admiralty had oversight of the great squadrons of the fleet, and busied itself with convoys and transports, inprests and embargoes, pirates, privateering, passes, and the enforcement of the trade laws." [25] Not until the latter part of the seventeenth century, however, did it become active in the protection of colonial trade. The Crown, the Privy Council, the Treasury and the Admiralty were represented in the colonies: the Crown and the Privy Council, by the governors and the naval officers; the Treasury, by the surveyor general and the collectors of customs; and

[22] Beer, G. L., *The Old Colonial System*, Part I, Vol. 1, p. 262.
[23] *Ibid.*, p. 260; Andrews, C. M., *The Colonial Period*, p. 133.
[24] Beer, G. L., *The Old Colonial System*, Part I, Vol. I, p. 260.
[25] Andrews, C. M., *The Colonial Period*, p. 133.

the Admiralty, both by "the vice-Admirals and the officers of the Admiralty Courts, which had cognizance of specific violations of the commercial system," and by "the captains and other officers of the royal navy, who were authorized under the Navigation Act to seize vessels violating certain of its provisions." [26]

In addition to these departments, with their committees and boards, an important body, so far as the colonies were concerned, was the Board of Trade and Plantations which was organized in 1696 as the successor of the former councils and committees. It was the duty of this Board to furnish information to the other bodies concerning the colonies. Andrews tells us that "the Board of Trade was the only important body in the British system of government that had no executive powers of its own. The Board lasted for eighty-seven years; it developed fairly definite ideas as to what the British policy toward the colonies should be; it maintained in the Plantation Office a permanent staff of secretaries and clerks who became the guardians of the traditions of the office, and upheld, during periods of political manipulation and frequent change, a more or less fixed colonial program." [27]

The Acts of Trade and Navigation. There were three acts of prime importance governing trade and navigation between England and the colonies during the seventeenth century. In 1651, after her civil war was over, England made her first real attempt to gain the supremacy of the seas. Holland at that time was her most potent rival; Spain had been humbled, and Cromwell had made an alliance with Portugal. The Navigation Act of 1651, then, was passed by England in an effort to strike a blow at Holland's carrying trade.

[26] Beer, G. L., *The Old Colonial System*, Part I, Vol. I, pp. 291–292.
[27] Andrews, C. M., *The Colonial Period*, p. 136.

The main provisions of this act were as follows:

I. "No goods of the growth or manufacture of Asia, Africa, or America shall be imported into England or the dominions thereof, except in ships of which the proprietor, master and the major part of the mariners are English.

II. "No goods of the growth or manufacture of Europe shall be imported into England or the dominions thereof, except in English ships and in such foreign ships as so belong to that country where the goods are produced and manufactured.

III. "No goods of foreign growth or manufacture, that are to be brought into England, shall be brought from any other place than the place of growth or production, or from those ports where alone the goods can be shipped, or whence they are usually first shipped after transportation.[28]

There were a few minor exceptions to these provisions; in case of violation of these acts, vessel and cargo were to be confiscated.

Although this act had little effect upon plantation trade, it marked the beginning of a series of such acts which did affect the colonies: the Navigation Act of 1660, for example, was instrumental in causing a great advance in the development of the merchant marine of England. One of its clauses provided that commerce between England and the colonies must be carried on in English-built ships with a crew three-fourths English. The effect of this act upon navigation at this time was so profound that the act was often referred to as the Great Charter of the Sea. There were two main principles involved in the

[28] Beer, G. L., *The Commercial Policy of England toward the American Colonies,* pp. 31-32.

Act of 1660: foreign shipping was discouraged and in some cases forbidden, while it was made difficult for foreigners to obtain supplies of raw materials, produced by English colonies. The underlying purpose of the act was to promote national power by increasing English sea forces and by expanding commerce, an aim which had been greatly hampered by the Dutch since the beginning of the seventeenth century. With the exception of one clause, the effect of the Navigation Act of 1660 was in general only a repetition of earlier attempts made during the reigns of the Stuarts. This clause was original in its exact enumeration of certain articles produced in the colonies; and provided for the forfeiture of vessel and contents in case these articles were shipped to any country other than Ireland, England or her colonies. The products enumerated were sugar, tobacco, cotton-wool, indigo, ginger and dyeing-woods, all of which came from the West Indies with the exception of tobacco which was produced in Virginia and Maryland. England enumerated those products which were to be used at home and in the colonies to make her independent of her rivals in Europe. Ships sailing from England or Ireland to the colonies, or bringing in products from the colonies to England, were forced to give bonds of £1000 or £2000, depending upon their tonnage. Beer says that "the effect of the Act was to give English, Irish and colonial shipping a monopoly of the carrying trade within the Empire, and to make England the staple for tobacco and the West Indian products." [29] This would naturally operate to bring England and her colonies into closer contact.

In 1663 England passed the "Staple Act" prohibiting European commodities from being imported into the colonies unless shipped from England. There were a few

[29] Beer, G. L., *The Old Colonial System*, Part I, Vol. I, p. 76.

exceptions to this rule for articles of consumption prohibited in England; for instance: wines from the Ma-
deiras, a possession of Portugal, one of the allies of
England, were permitted to be shipped directly to the
colonies. After a time the disadvantages which arose in
connection with the shipping of commodities from one
colony to another aroused criticism; the colonies had
either light duties or no import duties to pay, but on
goods shipped to England, customs duties were demanded. It is not surprising, therefore, that the colonies
preferred to ship products to one another. Moreover, when a product was sent into England and again
exported from that country, only a part of the duty collected there was repaid. Thus the colonies conforming
to these regulations were at an obvious disadvantage when
selling commodities in a foreign country, as compared
with those colonies which violated the law and shipped
products directly.

As a result of the dissatisfaction aroused by this in-
equity, Parliament made an investigation of the question,
and in 1673 passed a statute which required export duties
to be paid upon the products enumerated in the Act of
1660, when shipped from one colony to another, such
duties to be levied upon the basis of the subsidy of 1660.
In this group, tobacco and sugar were the most important
commodities. The duty on raw sugar at one shilling and
sixpence per hundred weight was considerable, the duty
of one penny per pound on tobacco was, on the other
hand, only half the English duty of 1660. While this
bill was ostensibly a revenue measure, it was imposed
primarily to prevent infringement of the enumeration
stipulations in the Act of 1660, and the small amount of
revenue which resulted from its passage was of minor
consequence. After duties had been paid on com-

modities, the latter were liable to the enumeration rules, and were not allowed to be transported directly to foreign parts. There was some controversy concerning this provision, but in 1696 a law was passed which dispelled any doubt upon the point.

Beer asserts that three acts passed by Parliament—the Navigation Act of 1660, the Staple Act of 1663, and the Plantation Duties Act of 1673—formed the basis for the entire economic structure of the colonial system.[30] Underlying these statutes were the two fundamental principles: that English commerce must be carried on in English ships, and that certain enumerated articles must be shipped to England.[31] This was an expression of British mercantilism.

The English Customs and Revenue System. With the acquisition of her colonial possessions England was confronted with the necessity of establishing rules governing the financial relations between herself and these minor bodies. From the beginning the colonies were regarded as external to the English fiscal realm. Upon their commodities when imported into England duties were levied, and duties were imposed in England upon goods when sent to the colonies. Had the colonies not been restrained by England in their relations, they would have been influenced to a certain extent by these customs, but England on her side, would not have been so closely in touch with colonial finances. The Staple Act of 1663, with the clauses specifying certain articles to be taxed according to the import and export duties of England, played an important part in shaping economic conditions in the colonies. The most momentous of the statutes embodied in these laws was the "Old Subsidy" which placed a tax

[30] Beer, G. L., *The Old Colonial System*, Part I, Vol. I, p. 84.
[31] Connor, R. D. W., Lecture notes, February 25, 1927.

on imports and exports. By this Act of 1660 a tonnage and poundage subsidy was granted by Parliament to Charles II for life. The tonnage placed on imported wines was a specific duty; the poundage was supposed to be an ad valorem duty, equal to five per cent, which was placed on all imports and exports. Since the value of these goods was ascertained in a hit-or-miss manner, the duties on them rarely corresponded to five per cent of the actual value of the products: sometimes they were far in excess, and again they were below the duty of market value. These variations existed, for example, in the taxes on tobacco in the colonies. Beer tells us that "colonial tobacco was valued at twenty pence a pound, when it could be freely bought in Virginia and Maryland for from one penny to twopence, and sold in England, after paying duties, freight, and other charges, from four to five pence." [32] This tariff, alleged to be an ad valorem duty, was in reality a specific duty.

All exports to the colonies or to any country were, as a rule, subjected to a tax of five per cent. Such duties on exports, however, did not amount to any considerable revenue for England, for the "Book of Rates" usually placed them at a very low rate; nevertheless they could not be overlooked, especially from the English standpoint. England was at that time principally an agricultural country, and exported many products used for food. The incidence of these exports fell at different places according to the nature of outside rivalry; with direct competition of farm products from the colonies against English products in the market, the export duties were paid by the English farmers. On some manufactured products the duties were only partially shifted to the consumer in the colonies, and in cases where there was no

[32] Beer, G. L., *The Old Colonial System*, Part I, Vol. I, p. 130.

competitive commodity in the colonies, these export duties were entirely shifted to the colonial consumer.

In the matter of duties on imports into England, the tariff of 1660 rates the many products from the colonies for lower duties, thus discriminating against foreign products of a similar nature. Among these articles were tobacco, sugar, and cotton.[33] Tobacco from foreign parts was valued at ten shillings per pound, which made the five per cent called for in "Old Subsidy" amount to sixpence duty; colonial tobacco was valued at one shilling, eightpence per pound, which made the duty one penny, but another one penny was added to this duty, making a total duty of twopence.[34] On unrefined sugar from foreign markets the duty was four shillings per hundred-weight, while the colonial rate was one shilling, sixpence; but on refined sugar, the difference was less.[35] Cotton from foreign countries paid fourpence per pound, while that from the English colonies paid no duty whatever.[36]

Since England was dominated by the agricultural element, the tariff of 1660 placed very high duties on imports of cereals and other farm products to that country as a protection to the English farmer. These duties did not affect the colonies, however, for it was not at that time possible for them to export such products to England; the duties were originated for the principal purpose of excluding Irish products. The preference which the tariff gave to the colonial enumerated commodities insured for the colonies a practical monopoly, as to the commodities, in the English market.[37] The incidence of these import duties, except in the cases where

[33] Beer, G. L., *The Old Colonial System*, Part I, Vol. I, p. 133.
[34] *Ibid.*, p. 134.
[35] *Ibid.*, p. 134.
[36] *Ibid.*, p. 134.
[37] *Ibid.*, p. 137.

they caused a decline in demand, fell on the English consumer and resulted in reduced consumption. Many of the commodities imported into England, however, were sent out to other countries to be consumed, and the duties on the products, in cases of this kind, were paid by the producer in the colony. Furthermore, the Staple Act of 1663 imposed a prohibition on the shipment of foreign products to the colonies unless such products were first sent to England and duty collected there. The effect of these laws, then, was to lay a direct tax in the colonies upon the people who produced and consumed such commodities. England, however, had passed an act in 1660 which guaranteed a refund of half duties upon commodities if they were reshipped from England within a certain period— usually from nine months to one year. In such cases the actual amount of duty received by England was two and one-half per cent instead of five. Beer states that "In the case of colonial tobacco—the most important item— not only was half of the subsidy repaid, but also the entire additional duty of one penny; the amount remaining in the English Treasury on Virginia tobacco re-exported from England to foreign markets was thus only a half penny a pound."[38]

Tobacco was the only item in the "enumerated products" which could be grown in England, but preferential duties could not exert enough influence to keep English producers out of the market. England, therefore, prohibited the planting of tobacco in England and, prompted by the desire to promote the prosperity of the colonies, made serious and eventually successful efforts to enforce this law.[39]

[38] Beer, G. L., *The Old Colonial System*, Part I, Vol. I, p. 138.
[39] *Ibid.*, p. 150.
Some of the colonies, the West Indies, for example, were actively en-

The foundation of the revenue from English customs was laid by the "Old Subsidy" in 1660. Twenty-nine years later, when the French wars were raging, England was confronted with the necessity of raising money to defray expenses; consequently, at the beginning of George I's reign, the total duties on imports were equal in amount to at least three subsidies. Beer says that "apart from the tonnage duties on wines and other specific taxes, those duties were at that time equivalent to fifteen per cent of the rated value of the commodities imported." [40] There were, in addition, particular duties placed by Parliament when the occasion demanded. Many such instances occurred under Charles II and at the beginning of James II's reign when the duties on tobacco and sugar were raised to a considerable extent. Although some quit-rents from colonies were received before 1689 by the Crown, these were not important; their yield was often large but the King frequently gave them as a bounty to the colonies for some specific purpose. The records of that time show that England received practically no income directly from the colonies, and that when such revenue was received it was generally used for the purpose of fostering the welfare of the colonies. On the other hand, the colonies were only a small burden to the Crown, for each colony was encouraged to raise revenue to meet its own expenditures for local purposes.[41] This condition prevailed within the colonies at

gaged in the production of sugar. The question of taxing this product furnished some of the most important controversies of the day, and aroused opposition generally more vehement than that engendered by discussion of the tobacco tax. The sugar industry was more widespread and affected more types of trades than did the tobacco industry,—English merchants carrying on trade in Portugal and in the West Indies. The sugar refiners in England, and the sugar planters in the colonies were all opposed to any encroachment upon their profits.

[40] Beer, G. L., *The Old Colonial System,* Part I, Vol. I, p. 147.
[41] *Ibid.,* p. 202.

the close of the Restoration Period and was to remain practically constant until after the middle of the eighteenth century, when difficulties began to present themselves. The Seven Years' War, ending in 1762 in the Peace of Paris, left England with a heavy debt. The old land tax of four shillings in the pound, and other sources of revenue in the country could not produce returns sufficient to meet the needs occasioned by the debt; so an additional source of taxation was sought.[42]

Up to this time the American Colonies had not been taxed by England for revenue purposes. The general opinion existing in the colonies during this period on the subject of British taxation is interesting. The majority of the settlers in the colonies held their titles to the land by grants from the Crown, but after the Revolution, when the House of Commons acquired all jurisdiction over matters of taxation throughout Great Britain, the colonies considered their position in this matter altered. No true Whig in England would have conceded the exclusive right of the colonies to grant revenue to the King; while the colonies, in their turn, logically refused to admit the power of a representative assembly, like the House of Commons, to tax those who had no representation in that body. The colonies realized the advantages obtained from trade relations with the older country, and did not object to imposts for regulating trade; the right of Parliament, however, to impose taxes on goods to be sold in the country, unlike the customs duties, was not acknowledged by the colonies.[43]

During the Seven Years' War the American Colonies

[42] Dowell, S., *A History of Taxation and Taxes in England,* Vol. II, pp. 47, 48, 139.
[43] *Ibid.,* p. 147.

had developed with amazing rapidity.[44] Grenville, realizing the size of the national debt and the heaviness of the taxes and perplexed by the difficulty of finding new ways of obtaining revenue for the support of the standing army which he determined to maintain in the colonies, decided to tax the American Colonists. He proposed to collect customs duties at the ports of America and to levy an "internal tax" by means of duties similar to those levied in England and known as Stamp duties.[45] This proposal infuriated the colonies, so that when the Stamp Act arrived in America it was received with "universal disobedience and open resistance," [46] causing a hostile controversy between England and her American Colonies which was to last for over a decade. Burke, in a speech on March 22, 1775, said: "The public and avowed origin of this quarrel was on taxation." [47] His admonition to his English colleagues, on April 19, 1774, to "leave America, if she has a taxable matter in her, to tax herself" [48] was not heeded. England's opinion that she had the "right of taxing" [49] the colonies resulted in a declaration of independence by the colonies on July 4, 1776, followed by a war which validated this announcement.

Direct and Local Taxes in England. In addition to the levy of taxes on articles of consumption, as exemplified in her customs duties on exports and imports and her excise tax, England imposed a few direct taxes which should be considered in an attempt to obtain a complete

[44] Dowell, S., *A History of Taxation and Taxes in England,* Vol. II, p. 148.   [45] *Ibid.,* p. 149.

[46] Burke, E., *Observations on a late publication, The Present State of the Nations,* Works, Vol. III, p. 81.

[47] Burke, E., *Speech on Conciliation with the Colonies,* p. 59.

[48] *Ibid., Speech on American Taxation,* Vol. II, p. 72.

[49] Johnson, S., *Taxation No Tyranny,* p. 51.

picture of her taxation system for the purpose of suggesting its influence upon colonial taxation. Although direct taxes in England—unlike the customs duties—had no direct bearing upon taxation in the colonies, the imposition of such taxes suggested forms which the colonies might use to shape a revenue system. The settlers in North Carolina, Virginia, and South Carolina were predominantly English; it was natural, therefore, that North Carolina, as a colony of England, should draw inspiration for the method to be used in obtaining its revenue from the English practice.

During the war between Charles I and Parliament, after most of the silver in the kingdom had been utilized to finance this struggle, Parliament was compelled to seek other means of obtaining revenue for continuing the war. This necessity led to the authorization of a land tax, the development of which we shall review later. It was also during the civil war in 1643, that Parliament introduced a tax on the sale of a variety of articles of consumption. These articles were chiefly some brand of drinks, such as ale, beer, cider, and strong liquors. The following year other types of commodities were added, such as flesh, salt, alum, coperas, hops, starch, saffron, silks, caps and hats of various kinds.[50] This excise tax in 1647 was made a normal part of the fiscal system for all of these articles, except flesh and salt which were produced at home;[51] since it proved a success as a revenue-producing agent it remained in force, with modifications and extensions, during and after the period under discussion.

From the Restoration in 1660 to the Revolution in

[50] Dowell, S., *A History of Taxation and Taxes in England,* Vol. II, pp. 9, 12, 13, 14.
[51] *Ibid.,* p. 10.

1688, however, the only continuous direct tax in England was known as hearth money, a charge of two shillings imposed upon each hearth in every dwelling.[52]   At different times during this period for some specific purpose, such as carrying on war with Holland or with France, England resorted to several kinds of direct taxes, such as the poll or capitation taxes;[53] subsidies,[54] or the commonwealth form of monthly assessment upon property;[55] and a few unclassified sums levied in a special manner.[56]   These forms of taxation remained in existence only for defraying some particular expense; after this purpose was served, the tax automatically ceased.

The hearth money levy collected during the reign of Charles II was repealed a short time after the Revolution, to be succeeded, in 1696, by a fixed tax of two shillings on houses, with higher rates for homes containing more than a specified number of windows.[57] This latter tax remained in existence during and after the American colo-

---

[52] *Ibid.,* p. 29.

[53] Dowell, S., *A History of Taxation and Taxes in England,* Vol. II, pp. 31, 32. "The first poll, in 1660, produced £252,167.   Another in 1666, for the purposes of the Dutch War, about £500,000; while a third in 1667 for the preparations against France in the Act which prohibited the importation of French goods, produced about £150,000."

[54] *Ibid.,* pp. 32. "In 1663, four entire subsidies were granted by the temporality; and four subsidies, granted by the clergy, were confirmed by parliament in the ancient form. The subsidies produced about £282,000." This method of taxation was not reasonably remunerative and was never used again.

[55] Dowell, S., *A History of Taxation and Taxes in England,* Vol. II, pp. 32, 33.

[56] In 1670 a sum of £800,000 alloted to the King, was levied in a special manner, as follows: "By a rate of 15s in every £100 belonging to bankers, or lent to the King at above 6 percent; 6s in every £100 on all personal estates; 2s in the £ on the salaries of all offices and places; and 1s in the £ on lands and wines." Dowell, *A History of Taxation and Taxes in England,* Vol. II, p. 33.

[57] *Ibid.,* p. 54.

nial period, with rates increased from time to time whenever revenue was needed from this source. In 1709 the existing rate of ten shillings on all houses having twenty windows or more [58] was raised; and again in 1758 there was an increase in the house tax, with a new tax imposed upon income from offices.[59]

The land tax next claims attention. In 1688 there was a monthly assessment upon property, but a year later a rate was applied to income from personal property "taking 100 lbs. of value as equivalent to an income of £6" —income from offices and employments of profits, not naval or military—and "the yearly value of houses, land, quarries, wines, iron and salt works, and profits from land." [60] Assessments were made for specific amounts and charged to the particular localities where revenue was to be raised. From this time until the end of the century rates fluctuated between one shilling to four shillings to the pound upon general property.[61] Between 1689 and 1700 the personality tax was regularly evaded to such an extent that "the tax which was intended to rest in the first instance on goods and offices, the residue only being charged on the land—intended for a general tax on property, gradually became, in effect, a tax on land, and a most unfair one." [62] By 1702, the land tax, although granted annually, settled into a permanent tax, which, it was esti-

[58] The rates were "for houses with from 20 to 30 windows, 10s; and for houses with 30 or more windows, 20s." Dowell, S., *A History of Taxation and Taxes in England*, Vol. II, p. 75.

[59] Offices were already taxed 4s per pound. "The new duty was at the rate of 1s for all offices with a salary exceeding £100 except naval and military offices." Dowell, S., *A History of Taxation and Taxes in England*, Vol. II, p. 135.

[60] Dowell, S., *A History of Taxation and Taxes in England*, Vol. II, p. 50.

[61] *Ibid.*, p. 52.

[62] *Ibid.*, p. 53.

mated, produced at the rate of two shillings to the pound about a million of revenue during years of peace.[63]

In time of war the rate was usually increased to meet such particular expenses as the exigencies of the occasion demanded. During the war of the Spanish Succession this tax of two shillings was raised to four shillings, which rate was imposed annually throughout the war period.[64] In 1714, the year after the war had ceased, the tax was lowered to its normal rate of two shillings.[65]. In 1731, Walpole, in an attempt to win the attachment of the landed gentry to the House of Hanover, for the first time lowered the land tax to one shilling;[66] however, later in the decade it was again raised to two shillings. This rate remained in force until the latter part of 1739 when another war with Spain, growing out of the Right of Search, and also the war of the Austrian Succession necessitated additional funds. The land tax was then increased to four shillings, the maximum war rate.[67] After the Peace of Aix-La-Chapelle, in 1748, the land tax was again reduced, and in 1750 the charge was fixed at three shillings. By 1753, however, the rate had again reached its normal level of two shillings.[68] Such is the brief history of the land tax rate which prevailed in England during the time that North Carolina was an English colony.[69]

[63] Dowell, S., *A History of Taxation and Taxes in England*, Vol. II, p. 63.

[64] *Ibid.*, p. 71.

[65] *Ibid.*, p. 81.

[66] *Ibid.*, p. 99.

[67] *Ibid.*, p. 111.

[68] *Ibid.*, p. 125.

[69] *Ibid.*, p. 53. Dowell makes the statement that "this system of a grant of a certain sum as for a rate of 1s, 2s, 3s, or 4s, in the pound, for the particular year, continued its force down to 1798 when Pitt, before the introduction of his income tax, made the land tax at 4s, perpetual in the form of a redeemable rent charge on the various districts."

Rudimentary business and license taxes which played a rôle in English internal revenue may also have influenced similar developments which appeared in the colony of North Carolina. In 1694 a tax was imposed on the hackney coach business in London, which was in reality an extension of a license system, brought into practice during the reign of Charles I, for allowing hackney coachmen to operate in the city.[70] A license tax of four pounds or more, dependent upon the number of animals required for carrying purposes, was in 1697 placed upon the trade of hawkers and peddlars.[71] In 1714 this tax with an increased rate was still in force in England. To these license taxes were added from time to time others of a similar or miscellaneous character, such as the tax on the possession of plate, cards and dice, in 1756, and that on deeds, newspapers and advertisement, in 1757.[72] Other miscellaneous taxes, such as those on bachelors, burials, births and marriages, imposed in 1695, were less permanent but serve nevertheless to illustrate the general nature of this factor in the tax system of England during the seventeenth and eighteenth centuries.[73]

Since the poll tax was used to a considerable extent as a method of obtaining revenue in North Carolina, especially during the latter part of the colonial period, it is interesting to note the slight part which this tax played in the English taxation system. As in North Carolina, the poll tax in England was imposed only for meeting

[70] "Every hackney coachman was now required to take out a license for which he paid £5 and subsequently an annual rent of £4, the number of licenses being limited to 700." Dowell, S., *A History of Taxation and Taxes in England,* Vol. II, p. 54.

[71] Dowell, S., *A History of Taxation and Taxes in England,* Vol. II, p. 54.

[72] *Ibid.,* p. 83.

[73] *Ibid.,* p. 65.

extraordinary expenses. The first English poll tax was levied in 1660, three years before Albemarle became an organized colony, the next one being imposed in 1666. The purpose of this levy was to supply revenue to meet the expenses of waging war against the Dutch. Eleven years later, in 1677, the third poll tax was levied in England in order to carry on war against France.[74] The revenue from these three levies having proved reasonably satisfactory, William III attempted to use the poll tax during part of his reign but it was not so remunerative as he had anticipated. It was therefore abandoned altogether in England as a source of revenue. The first poll tax of William III was imposed in 1689; two additional ones were placed upon his subjects in 1690; while from 1692 through 1698, with exception of the two years 1695 and 1696, other taxes of this nature were levied.[75] By 1698, however, it was discovered to be very unproductive as a source of revenue, because evasions of the tax were notorious. Moreover, because this form of taxation bore more heavily upon the very poor than the subsidies or any other tax,[76] a popular antipathy toward it developed. The levy in 1698, therefore, was the last poll tax imposed in England during the period when North Carolina was a colony.

Before terminating a discussion of taxes in England, mention should be made of her local system of taxation; for there appears to be a similarity between the local system of taxation employed in England and that applied in the colony of North Carolina. During the period

[74] Dowell, S., *A History of Taxation and Taxes in England*, Vol. II, pp. 31, 32.

[75] *Ibid.*, p. 48.

[76] There is a lucid discussion of this subject in Dowell's, *History of Taxation and Taxes in England*, Vol. II, pp. 15–63.

under discussion local taxation in England centered around the poor rates;[77] in 1536, during the reign of Henry VIII, a law was passed requiring provision by public offering for the aid of the poor: "Not casual acts of charity, but regulated systematic largess, ordered and collected in accordance with the sections of an Act of Parliament."[78] Many reasons have been given for making this tax a local charge, chief of which seems to have been the fact that neighbors could acquire knowledge of each other's affairs easily, thereby affording a ready means of approximating equality in this burden.[79] "It was rightly recognized," states Row-Fogo, "that the administration of poor relief must always be conducted in the domain of local government. The local authorities were also the only available agents for raising money."[80]

The poor-rate in the parish was not assessed uniformly upon all inhabitants as an equal pound rate, but, according to an ancient custom, by the vestry "without respect to value, but according to the ability of the party charged, such ability being estimated with reference to property, whether in the parish or out of it."[81] This was usually a tax placed on land according to its value.[82] During the first fifty years of the eighteenth century, the "usage of not taxing men in respect of movables, or of taxing them at an absurdly low rate became so confirmed in many parishes that the judges hesitated to upset it by a clear declaration of the law."[83] The statute books showed

[77] Cannan, E., *The History of Local Rates in England*, p. 2; p. 102.
[78] Row-Fogo, J., *Local Taxation in England*, p. 68.
[79] *Ibid.*, p. 34.
[80] *Ibid.*, p. 67.
[81] Cannan, E., *The History of Local Rates in England*, p. 79.
[82] *Ibid.*, p. 80.
[83] *Ibid.*, p. 90.

laws in favor of taxing personal property but these laws seem to have been disregarded in practice.[84]

Other local rates were imposed for various purposes from time to time, conspicuous among them, the church-rate. In 1647, however, Long Parliament passed an act in which the church-rate was united with the local rate.[85] In actual practice this ordinance was not always enforced.[86] All the minor Tudor statutory rates gradually tended to merge with the poor-rate, with ability as the standard to be used in assessment.[87] Finally, in 1739, during the reign of George II, all of these rates were consolidated and amalgamated with the poor-rate.[88]

As compared with the American Colonies, England was a highly civilized country during the seventeenth and eighteenth centuries. The method of building roads in England where the cost of construction was met by the proceeds of taxation, differed from the primitive method of North Carolina where roads were built through the personal services of people living in the neighborhood. An act introduced in England in 1654 provided for a body of landholders from each parish to meet and levy a tax for roadbuilding purposes. The rates might vary according to the local needs but at this time the maximum limit for all the rates in any one locality was twelvepence per pound per year.[89] During the latter part of the seventeenth century these assessments were not permitted to exceed sixpence per pound for each year,[90] and were to be laid on the

---

[84] Cannan, E., *The History of Local Rates in England,* pp. 88, 93.

[85] *Ibid.,* p. 104.

[86] *Ibid.,* p. 105.

[87] *Ibid.,* p. 109. These minor rates were for bridges, for jails, for houses of correction, for prisoners in the King's Bench and in County jails, and for paying the cost of conveying vagabonds, and others.

[88] *Ibid.,* pp. 109, 110.

[89] *Ibid.,* p. 119.

[90] *Ibid.,* pp. 121, 122.

same taxpayers and in the same proportion as the poor-rate.[91]   It was not until 1767 that the highway rate was merged with the poor-rate.[92]   Cannan tells us that "in general, the rates for street expenditure, such as paving, cleansing, watering, lighting, and watching, created by local acts, seem to have conformed closely to the poor-rate though there were many differences on points of detail." [93]   The poor-rate with these various assimilated rates, thus seems to have provided the system of local taxation in England during this period.

The Colony of North Carolina; the Changed Economy and Taxation. How, then, did England with her taxation system as described above, influence the mode of taxation in North Carolina?   England passes under review as a mighty political unit destined to be one of the most powerful empires in the world.   The country, during that period, enjoyed the cultural and economic advantages belonging to a state in the vanguard of civilization; houses of the finest construction of the day; highways financed and built by the state; cities with all the advantages of an advanced industrial system, herald of the capitalistic era to follow; a taxation system on which not a little effective thought had been expended; these were some of the salient evidences of England's internal economy.

The Colony of North Carolina appears in contrast, but with the inherent capacity for development of these essential characteristics.   During the earlier part of this period the territory was nothing more than a vast wilderness with a body of settlers organized into a small colony on the coast.   Gradually the settlement grew and other settlements were made, so that by the end of the colonial

---

[91] Canaan, E., *The History of Local Rates in England*, p. 122.
[92] *Ibid.*, p. 122.
[93] *Ibid.*, pp. 129, 130.

period a loose net-work of colonists covered this do-main. Living conditions were crude, the prevailing type of house being built out of roughly hewn logs, and, even toward the end of the period, there were only a very few homes, built of material imported from Eng-land, which could in any manner approximate Eng-lish houses. There were no highways, and the few miserable roads had been built by the manual labor of the settlers. There were no cities, and a few families, living at a convenient place for trade, formed the only concentrated groupings of people in this rural region. The industrial system, which was crude, individual, and self-sufficing, has been likened to the manorial or house-hold systems which preceded the domestic system in Eng-land. Here was truly a "forest primeval." In this area, with its primitive economy, England attempted to implant her culture with its attendant economy. Naturally this setting, to which such a system was to be transplanted, would modify the various elements composing the original pattern; necessity caused the colony to assimilate some aspects of this economy, usually with modifications, while it rejected others.

The taxation system in the colony was a phase of the economic system which conformed to the general rule of change. Some parts of the English system were used as models in levying taxes in North Carolina, while others were ignored or supplemented according to the needs of the colony. The land tax, which played a very important rôle in the internal taxation system of England, was almost negligible in the colonial finances of North Carolina. It was used for only a brief time for a specific purpose and then abandoned altogether until the colony declared its independence. This seeming peculi-arity is accounted for by historians in the quit-rents, a feudal due collected from landowners in the colony by the agents of the King of England. This due usurped the place of a land tax, because, as the land was considered to have borne its share of public financial burdens, no tax on it was deemed advisable.

Among other sources from which support was sought for the political organization of the colony were the customs duties,—taxes placed on imports and exports. The customs were a part of the British colonial system of taxation, and, as such, touched every colony. It is interesting to note the twofold aspect of this system in its relation to North Carolina in the regulations imposed by England and in those formulated by the colony itself. Probably the most conspicuous form of taxation in North Carolina during this era was the poll tax. In England, as shown above, the poll tax played a very minor part at this time, being used only during the latter half of the seventeenth century, while in North Carolina its course can be traced clearly during the eighteenth century. Then, again, the influence on trade of the English business and license taxes—if they may be so called—was evident in North Carolina during the latter part of the colonial period as will be seen in a later chapter.

Local taxes in England were reflected in the North Carolina colony. Church tithes and poor-rates existed in both societies, with the church tithes in North Carolina predominating and the poor-rate in England holding the center of the stage during this period. As North Carolina was in the process of construction, she had need of many new buildings in which to conduct affairs of government; taxes for the purpose of building court houses in the various localities were therefore imposed. This was a necessity in North Carolina not common under the already established government of England. Thus the range of taxes prevalent in North Carolina developed during the time when that region was a colonial possession of England. These taxes did not appear in a well-constructed and considered system but were the spontaneous exactions of a primitive society at specific times and according to any method which proved effective for meeting the demand of the occasion. From this glance at the background of English thought and from this study of the English financial conditions, which exerted an almost incalculable influence upon the colony, we may pass to a direct consideration of taxation in North Carolina during the colonial period. A survey of the taxation system in that colony is the object of the following chapters.

Chapter II

Q U I T - R E N T S

ORIGIN. Although quit-rents were not considered a tax according to the technical definition of the term, they were a type of feudal due which cannot be ignored in any history of taxation in an area in which they were collected. The quit-rent system, an inextricable phase of the land system, was an English institution transported to American soil. As a part of the manorial system, it was a feudal due which originated in the first money payment required by the lord from the tenant, in place of the payment formerly made in kind or in labor. This rent, which the landlord received from the occupants of his land, bore the name suggestive of its meaning, for by the payment of the quit-rent, the tenant was quit, i.e., free from all other annual feudal charges.[1] There appear to be two theories concerning the origin of the term quit-rent,[2]

[1] Bond, B. W., *The Quit-Rent System in the American Colonies,* p. 25.

[2] a. Blackstone, *Commentaries,* Vol. II, p. 42. "Certain established rents of the freeholders and ancient copy-holders of a manor" . . . were . . . "denominated quit-rents, *quieti reditus;* because thereby the tenant goes quit and free of all other services. When these payments were reserved in silver or white money, they were anciently called 'white rents,' or 'blanch forms' *reditus albi,* in contradistinction to rents reserved in work, grain or baser money, which were called *reditus nigri* or blackmaild."

b. Palgrave, *Dictionary of Political Economy,* Vol. III, p. 249. A. E. Stamp in his article on the Quit-Rent defines it as a "small annual payment, formerly made by the tenants of a manor in commutation of all customary services and payments in kind. Quit-rent was sometimes

neither of which invalidates Bond's statement. Payable at first, to the Lord Proprietors who owned North Carolina, and later to the King who purchased it, the quit-rents were a symbol of the colony's feudal dependence.

A clear conception of the significance of quit-rents in North Carolina cannot be obtained without a review of their origin and growth in England. In that country quit-rents were a result of the attempt to convert the peasants of both types, free tenants and villeins,[3] into "freeholders and copyholders"[4] who were required to pay their rents in a relatively stable sum of money from year to year. With the increased supply of coined money the old method of payment in products and in labor had not only become awkward and ineffective, but also creative of much friction between the lord and his tenants. It was gradually becoming the fashion everywhere to use money for payments of all sorts. The exhaustion of the land in England, according to Professor Simkhovitch, resulted in the movement of the population from the rural districts to the centers of industry in towns and seaports;[5] the old manorial system disintegrated, "enclosures" for pasturage appeared; money wages came into existence, and the remaining farm peasants progressed to a higher stage of economic development, with a more

written White-Rent, whence some antiquaries have maintained that quit-rents were paid in silver: 'white' is, however, probably nothing but a phonetic variation of 'quit.'"

[3] Blackstone, *Commentaries,* Vol. II, p. 61. Bracton, a writer during the rule of Henry III of England says "Tenements are of two kinds, 'frank tenements' and 'villenage.' And of 'frank tenements some are held freely in consideration of homage and knight-service; others in free socage with the service of fealty only.'"

[4] Bond, B. W., *The Quit-Rent System in the American Colonies,* p. 26.

[5] *See* Simkhovitch, V. G., *Toward the Understanding of Jesus and Other Historical Studies; also* Bradley, H., *The Enclosures in England, an Economic Reconstruction,* pp. 13, 35, 102–107.

stable legal basis. The free tenants, called freemen and sokemen,[6] who always had relatively few labor services to perform, were the first to transform their dues into money payments, and the chief attributes of a socage[7] tenure then became a fixed rent and fealty. The villeins, holding an inferior rank among the peasantry, and retaining their lands at the pleasure of the lord who demanded a great percentage of their farm products and exacted from them burdensome labor services upon his demesne, were retarded in their ability to transfer these old obligations into money payments.

It should not be erroneously assumed that this transposition of feudal services into feudal money dues had an uninterrupted and unbroken course. The movement was in fact vacillating and indefinite, swayed at all times by various influences. Bond says, "In some cases the commutation was only apparent, as when services were entered on the manor rolls in terms of money merely as a convenient form of reckoning; in others it was only temporary, as when the lords found opportunities to return to the old system after commutation had proved or seemed to have proved disadvantageous; still, again, it often became permanent only in part, as when the villein paid in both labor and money."[8] The growth of trade and industry, however, gradually effected a change, for some medium of exchange was needed in this new phase of economic life. The old economic system, with its labor dues and payment in products, was discarded for the new

[6] Webster, *New International Dictionary.* "A man who is under the soke of another," or is under the jurisdiction of another.

[7] *Ibid.,* "The status, tenure, or holding of a sokeman." "The tenure was by service fixed in amount and kind, generally agricultural; but with later commutation, socage came to include also any such tenure paying a money rent only and not burdened with any military service."

[8] Bond, B. W., *The Quit-Rent System in the American Colonies,* p. 27.

type of money payment. This process of transformation began in England during the first half of the fourteenth century, before the time of the Black Death, and was not completed until the latter half of the fifteenth century.[9] By the seventeenth century the few traces of the old order remaining in England had no economic weight and practically all feudal dues were paid in stated money equivalents.

When the English claimed and settled territory in America, they brought with them England's feudal land system with its accompanying institution of quit-rents. Claiming the original proprietorship of all lands in the British Empire, the King had exclusive power to assign unoccupied lands to the possession of others. During the early period of its growth the Province of North Carolina was granted to a proprietary, who in turn, by a "process of subinfeudation"[10] retained quit-rents, the usual feudal dues in the land patents granted to tenants. The quit-rent in this colony, then, was in reality a feudal fee to be paid by the freeholders of land whose term of holding was in free and common socage.[11] When the Crown later bought this land from the proprietary possessors, the feudal relations were more simplified, and, in the case of both proprietors and crown, attested to the "royal feudal supremacy"[12] in the colonial land system.

[9] Vinogradoff, P., *Villainage in England,* pp. 297, 307–312, 329.

[10] Bond, B. W., *The Quit-Rent System in the American Colonies*, p. 30.

[11] Blackstone, *Commentaries*, p. 61: "Where the service was not only free but certain, as by fealty only, by rent and fealty, etc. that tenure was called *liberum socagium,* or free socage. Those were the only freeholdings or tenements; the others were villeinous or servile." Webster says that free and common socage (by service of an honorable nature) came to include any free tenure not spiritual, military, nor serviential, as opposed to *villein socage* (be services not of an honorable nature) which included copyhold tenures and tenures by ancient demesne.

[12] Bond, B. W., *The Quit-Rent System in the American Colonies*, p. 30.

The transposal of the quit-rent charges on land in the colonies naturally caused much discussion among the settlers. In England the landholders accepted the quit-rents as an escape from payments in services and products, and, because through long usage they had become accustomed to this system, its justice or injustice was not questioned. In the colonies, however, the quit-rent was not symbolic of an escape from more odious charges, but in most cases was regarded as a capricious and imperious charge upon land. Ignoring the expense which the proprietors and Crown had incurred in establishing these colonies, the settlers usually claimed that the quit-rents were a charge for which they received nothing. The general English laws concerning quit-rents were supposed to be in effect in the American Colonies, but in actual practice this was not true. Distance was a hindrance to the enforcement of law so that, as a rule, each colony had specific laws regarding its particular problems,—for example, questions regarding the amount, the medium, the place and time of payment, and the method of enforcing these payments.

"The establishment of this land charge in the American Colonies," writes Bond, "was, therefore, in reality an attempt to transfer a feudal relationship and a feudal obligation from the old world, where it had a meaning, to the new where it had none." [13]

History. All lands in America discovered by English subjects were considered feudal possessions of the King of England; he had the right to confer these various territories upon persons of his choice who were granted the privilege of holding them in liege. These liege lords, in their turn, made grants of land to settlers. As late as

[13] Bond, B. W., *The Quit-Rent System in the American Colonies,* p. 34.

1662 the Albemarle settlers, by order of the English King, were required to hold their lands under the "Laws of Virginia." [14]   Some friends of the King, believing that this land presented colorful prospects as a profitable business enterprise, asked for a grant of this region and all other lands which lay below Virginia.   There were eight of these men to whom the King, Charles II, in 1663, granted "all that territory or tract of land, situated, lying and being within our dominions of America," extending from "six and thirty degrees" to "one and thirty degrees with latitude," and from the Atlantic Ocean "to the West as far as the South Seas." [15]   The charter stipulated further that the grantees were to "erect, incorporate and ordain the same into a province, and call it the Province of Carolina." [16]   These eight grantees, afterwards known as the Lords Proprietors of Carolina, held supreme power with allegiance to the King.   By their charter they were endowed with the privilege of possessing, using, exercising and enjoying "the same rights, jurisdictions, privileges, prerogatives, royalties, liberties, immunities, and franchises," and "in an ample manner, as any Bishop of Durham in our Kingdom of England theretofore" had "held, used, or enjoyed, or, of right ought, or could, have use or enjoy." [17]   They could hold this land "in free and common socage, and not in capite or by Knight's service: [18]

---

[14] Connor, R. D. W., *History of North Carolina*, p. 27.

[15] *Colonial Records,* Vol. I, p. 21.

[16] *Ibid.,* p. 23.

[17] *Ibid.,* p. 22.

[18] Bouvier's *Law Dictionary,* Baldwin's Century Edition, p. 641.   "A species of feudal tenure which differed very slightly from a pure and perfect feud, being entirely of a military nature; and it was the first, most universal, and most honorable of the feudal tenures.   To make a tenure by Knight-Service, a determinate quality of land was necessary

yielding and paying yearly" to the King, "for there came the yearly rent of twenty marks [19] of lawful money of England"—the first payment to be two years thence at the time of the feast of All Saints in 1665—"and also the fourth part of all gold or silver ore which within the limits aforesaid, shall from time to time happen to be found." [20]

The Lords Proprietors, in their turn, wished to plant settlements of people on this tract of land for the purpose of obtaining pecuniary remuneration. In spite of their declaration that their reason for settling the colony was "a laudable and pious zeal for the propagation of the Christian faith, and the enlargement of"—their—"empire and dominions," [21] the desire for individual gain was undoubtedly the real reason. Although the proprietors did not expect speedy returns, they were making a long-time investment in Carolina and expected their estates ultimately to receive considerable profits from this source. It was their intention to entice people to come from England and the other English colonial possessions in order to locate in Carolina. By the terms of their charter, upon the Lords Proprietors "at their will and pleasure" was conferred the prerogative of granting "the premises or any part or parcels thereof, to him or them that shall be willing to purchase the same, and to such person or persons as they shall think fit, to have and to hold, to them, the said person or persons, their heirs or assigns, in fee

---

which was called a knight's fee (q.v.) (feodurn militaire) the measure of which was estimated at twelve plough-lands."

[19] Bouvier's *Law Dictionary*, Baldwin's Century Edition, p. 757. "The English mark is two-thirds of a pound sterling, or 13s. 4d."

[20] *Colonial Records,* Vol. I, pp. 22, 23.

[21] *Ibid.,* p. 21.

simple [22] or fee tayle; [23] or for term of life, or lives, or years." [24]

Concurrently with their expressed desire for the introduction and the diffusion of English subjects in the colony, the Lords Proprietors on August 25, 1663, issued a pamphlet entitled "A Declaration and Proposal to All that Will Plant in Carolina." [25] Section 7 of that declaration states the following conditions of grant: "We will grant to every present undertaker for his own head, one hundred acres of land, to him and his heirs forever, to be held in free and common socage; and for every man-servant that he shall bring or send thither, that is fit to bear arms, armed with a good firelock musket, performed bore, twelve bullets to the pound, and with twenty pounds of bullets, fifty acres of land; and for every woman-servant thirty acres; and to every man-servant that shall come within that time, ten acres after the expiration of his time." [26] The section is concluded summarily with the following adjunct: "Note that we intend not hereby to be obliged to give the proportions of land above mentioned to masters and servants, longer than the first five years, to commence at the beginning of the first settlement." [27] The recipients of this offer were to transmit to

[22] Bouvier's *Law Dictionary*, p. 405: "An estate of inheritance"—"It is where lands are given to a man and to his heirs absolutely, without any end or limitation put to the estate."

[23] *Ibid.*, p. 405: Old English spelling of fee-tail, which signified "An inheritable estate which can descend to certain classes of heirs only.— The estate itself is said to have been derived from the Roman system of restricting estates.—An estate-tail may be general, i.e., limited to a special class of such heirs, e.g., heirs male or heirs female, or those begotten of a certain wife named."

[24] *Colonial Records*, Vol. I, p. 28.

[25] *Ibid.*, p. 43.

[26] *Ibid.*, p. 45.

[27] *Ibid.*, p. 45.

the Lords Proprietors, for the use of the land, a periodical payment designated by the term quit-rents. The Lords Proprietors stated the matter thus: "In consideration of the premises, we do expect by way of acknowledgement, and towards the charge we have been and shall be at, one half-penny for every acre that shall be granted as aforesaid, within the time before limited and expressed." [28] This charge of a half-penny for each acre, or four shillings and twopence for each hundred acres, was to be paid annually.

Two years later, in 1665, a second charter was granted to the Lords Proprietors with many provisions of the original charter, but enlarging the domain of Carolina on the north to "the degrees of thirty-six and thirty minutes, north latitude," and on the south "as far as the degrees of twenty-nine, inclusive, of north latitude." [29] The Lords Proprietors, in 1667, directed the Governor of Albemarle "to make grants of land within his province upon the following conditions, viz: every Freeman or Freewoman being Master and Mistress of a Family was to have 60 acres for themselves, 60 for every man-servant capable of bearing arms, and 50 for every other servant, and every servant was to have 50 acres for themselves at the expiration of their servitude and all grantees of land were to pay ½d per ann:[30] per acre quit-rent." [31]

Not all lands, however, were held originally by grant from the Lords Proprietors under the terms of the Declaration of 1663. Although there were two colonies in North Carolina from which the state gradually developed

---

[28] *Colonial Records*, Vol. I, p. 46.
[29] *Ibid.,* p. 103.
[30] In modern parlance this would read "½ penny per year."
[31] *Colonial Records,* Vol. I, p. 93.

—"one on the River Roanoak (now called Albemarle River), and borders in Virginia; the other at Cape Fear two degrees more southerly," as a writer described them in 1666 [32]—the one on Cape Fear was not settled permanently until 1723. The settlement, in the northeastern section of the state was the only white settlement in existence at that time. Among the original settlers of this, two types of land grants prevailed: in the territory adjacent to Virginia, at a rent of one farthing for each acre, [33] the settlers received their titles from the Governor of Virginia, ratified by the Lords Proprietors in 1679; [34] the other type of grant was that, given by the Indians and held by the people in Albemarle, which later became Albemarle County. It was the people in this section who, becoming alarmed over the doubtful legality of their land titles, applied to the Lords Proprietors for some recognition of their titles. As a result of their supplications, the Lords Proprietors sent over a document destined to become one of the most important agreements in the history of the colonial period in North Carolina; this was the "Great Deed of Grant," dated May, the first, 1668. [35] In this document the Albemarle settlers were given permission to hold their land upon the same conditions "as in Virginia which is two shillings for every hundred acres," [36] payable at the house of the tenant "in tobacco at one penny per pound, as appears by the law of that colony." [37]

A year later, in 1669, Locke drew up The Fundamental Constitutions, a set of rules and regulations

---

[32] *Colonial Records,* Vol. I, pp. 155, 156.

[33] The farthing was about one-fourth of a penny at that time.

[34] *Colonial Records,* Vol. I, p. 238.

[35] *Colonial Records,* Vol. III, p. 479.

[36] *Ibid.,* p. 480.

[37] *Colonial Records,* Vol. IV, p. 109.

by which the Lords Proprietors were to govern the colony of North Carolina. The law concerning the rents is expressed in Article 113 of this paper: "Whosoever shall possess any freehold in Carolina, upon what title or whatsoever, shall at the farthest, from and after the year one thousand six hundred and eighty-nine, pay yearly into the Lords Proprietors, for each acre of land, English measure, as much fine silver as is at this present time in one English penny, or the value thereof, to be as a chief rent and acknowledgment to the Lords Proprietors, their heirs and successors forever. And it shall be lawful for the palatine's count by their officers, at any time, to take a new survey of any man's land, not to oust him or any part of his possessions but that by such a survey, the just number of acres he possesseth may be known, and the rent thereon due, may be paid by him." [38]

There appear to have been exceptions to the rule of selling lands with a quit-rent at a half-penny per acre attached, as originally announced by the Lords Proprietors. As early as 1694 there is a record of their commissioning Archdale, the governor, to lease lands in one part of the colony for one shilling the hundred acres while in other parts the same quantity of land was to be sold at four shillings and twopence. [39] Another proviso stated that the governor might sell the lands north of Cape Fear at any rate of quit-rent which he might think desirable, provided the amount should not be less than a half-penny per acre.

"The said governor had, likewise, a power of granting lands reserving a quit-rent of ½d per acre per ann: upon all lands in the Southward of Albemarle County." [40] In 1702, when Sir Nathaniel Johnson was appointed Gov-

[38] *Colonial Records,* Vol. I, pp. 204, 205.
[39] *Ibid.,* Vol. I, pp. 390, 391; Vol. V, p. 94.
[40] *Ibid.,* Vol. V, p. 94.

ernor of Carolina "the like power of selling and granting lands upon the same terms of conditions" was conferred upon him.[41]

The settlers who migrated to North Carolina came for the purpose of obtaining land. As each family naturally took as much real estate as possible, this practice resulted in the concentration of large tracts of land in eastern North Carolina in the hands of a comparatively few families. In order to encourage the entrance of more people into the state and to prevent the accumulation of very large estates by a few, the Lords Proprietors, in 1708, informed Governor Cary that he was to allow no individual to take possession of more than six hundred and forty acres of land, which, of course, was to be leased at a half-penny per acre in quit-rents.[42] In 1715, the Lords Proprietors, noticing that settlement had not been rapid within North Carolina, began to offer inducements to attract new settlers. With this idea in view, an act for a more speedy settlement of the land was passed by the Assembly during its session that year, together with another act exempting new comers, for the term of one year, from the payment of levies; [43] the rate, however, remained the same. The settlers in North Carolina never objected to having quit-rents levied upon their lands, as did the large plantation owners in Virginia. There were many other phases of the subject, however, which caused much discussion and often serious agitation within the colony. Disputes arose concerning such questions as rates—by whom should they be determined; what should they be;

---

[41] *Colonial Records,* Vol. V, p. 94.

[42] *Ibid.,* Vol. V, p. 94.

[43] *The State Records of North Carolina* (Laws), Vol. XXV, pp. 120, 121, 159.

where and how should they be paid? Such discussions
were prevalent in North Carolina during the greater part
of the colonial period. Shortly after the Crown bought
the state from the Lords Proprietors, there arose the clas-
sical quit-rents quarrel which threatened to wreck the Government and brought anarchy for a time to one section of
the state. Although the Lords Proprietors had organized
a system for the collection of quit-rents and had secured
its sanction by an act of the Assembly, the prospect of
the smooth working of the system was not promising.
The Assembly had decided that the income from this
source should be used to pay the salaries of local officials,
but disorder, resulting from a large amount of arrears in
the collection of quit-rents, gave rise to complications.

The quit-rent system and the land system in North
Carolina were inextricably entangled. Under the Great
Deed to Albemarle the inhabitants claimed that their
lands should be held upon the same terms as those upon
which the Virginia inhabitants held theirs, but the Lords
Proprietors had never entirely acquiesced in this interpretation. Then, too, after the land office in Carolina
was closed in 1712, the legality of many patents, which
had been issued without the knowledge of the Lords Proprietors, became questionable. To the people owning the
patents, it was obvious that if the Crown approved these
grants, the quit-rents would be two shillings per 100 acres,
but if the grants were not approved, any amount which
the royal government might dictate would be levied upon
them. Moreover, the collection of arrears in quit-rents
from landlords who had paid none for years was likely to
be a duty not easily performed. The Crown, tactlessly
attempting to override all of these objections, and heed-
less of Governor Burrington's advice, increased the quit-

rents to four shillings per 100 acres and demanded that all payments be made in proclamation money rather than in commodities; [44] this started the trouble.

When George II bought North Carolina and South Carolina in 1729,[45] it is probable that no quit-rents had been collected in this territory for a long time; in fact, in the aggregate there was a large amount of rent which had never been collected from the two states. The King, in purchasing the land, gave to the Lords Proprietors £500 for these quit-rents in arrears, but when he had this matter brought before the General Assembly it was found that the settlers in North Carolina had paid most of their rents. The King thereupon offered to cancel all arrears of quit-rents in North Carolina on two conditions. The first proviso called upon the General Assembly to pass a law requiring all landowners to register all the lands which they owned, specifying the number of acres and their location, such record to be kept at the office of the Register of Deeds in each county. The purpose of this stipulation was to provide for the King a rent-roll which would furnish evidence and ensure a certain degree of accuracy in determining the rents. The second condition provided that all quit-rents and all officers' fees should be paid in specie [46] rather than in produce.[47]

Governor Burrington was sent over from England with this proclamation, but the House of Burgesses, in the Assembly, refused to pass such a law for the two following reasons:

[44] *Colonial Records,* Vol. III, pp. 78, 95–102.

[45] Ashe, S. A., *History of North Carolina,* Vol. I, p. 91.

[46] Proclamation Money.

[47] Only the Governor received a salary, but the other officers received fees.

1. The arrears of quit-rents in North Carolina were negligible.[48]
2. The regulation of quit-rents was a matter for the House of Burgesses to control, and not for the Governor. This precipitated a struggle between Governor Burrington and the House of Burgesses.[49]

This body stated in a message that "For nearly twenty years the officers' fees have been paid in paper currency at the rate mentioned in the Acts of Assembly" and these Acts take precedence over anything which the Governor might declare.[50]

The Governor replied that the instructions from the King repealed all previous laws concerning the payment of fees and several fiery debates thereupon ensued between Burrington and the House of Burgesses. The latter body refusing to obey, the matter was taken up again in 1734 by the next Governor, Gabriel Johnston. Johnston carefully refrained from mentioning how the quit-rents should be paid, but laid emphasis upon the place and the time of payment.[51] In 1735, however, he issued a proclamation requiring the quit-rents to be paid in gold and silver and establishing a place in the counties at which they should be paid. Theretofore collection had been made by the sheriff at the homes of the tenants, but the new order required the contributors to go to the sheriff. When they refused to do this Johnston issued a proclamation to the people stating that his "Majesty's Just Revenue" did not depend upon the approval of the Assembly. The Assembly, however, demanded that the King's col-

---

[48] Practically all the arrears of quit-rents at that time were to be found in South Carolina.

[49] *Colonial Records,* Vol. III, p. 294.

[50] *Ibid.,* Vol. III, p. 304.

[51] *Colonial Records,* Vol. IV, p. xiv.

lectors be arrested and brought before them for trial. Johnston finally offered a compromise and, in 1739, was instrumental in passing a law which was satisfactory to both sides. This law contained two distinct provisions: in the first place, it provided for a committee composed of the Governor, the members of the Council, the Receiver General, the Attorney-General, and the members of the House of Burgesses to meet and determine the value of paper money; in the second place, it provided for an increase in the number of places for collection of quit-rents.[52] The King, fearing that it might be detrimental to the interest of society for a group of mere men to determine the value of money, vetoed this law in 1740,[53] thereby renewing the contest.

The following year another effort to pass the quit-rent laws also failed, and between 1741 and 1748 the General Assembly refused to enact any other quit-rent laws. As an indication of their state of mind regarding this subject, an excerpt from the proposals of the General Assembly, in 1744 presents a vital picture.[54] This was embodied in the following passage resolving that "no produce of this province being accepted in payment of quit-rents of late years, nor the current bills at less than 10 for 1, which is equal to sterling money, as this from the great scarcity of silver and gold puts it entirely out of the power of the greatest part of the inhabitants of this province to pay their quit-rents being contrary to the Grand Deed and also of the law of this province is a very great grievance." [55] In 1748, however, by splitting the popular party, Johnston succeeded in

[52] *Colonial Records,* Vol. IV, p. xvii.
[53] Connor, R. D. W., *History of North Carolina,* Vol. I.
[54] *Colonial Records,* Vol. IV, p. xvii.
[55] *Ibid.,* p. xvii.

enacting the quit-rent law, or the "Act, for forming a Rent-Roll of all the lands holden in this province, for quieting inhabitants in their possessions and for directing the payment of quit-rents." [56]

In 1749, 1750 and 1754, similar acts were passed by the Assembly. In 1755, however, an act was signed which permitted the owners of land to use "inspector's notes for tobacco at 1d per lb.; or in indigo at 3d per lb." for the purpose of paying their quit-rents.[57] In a letter written on February 5, 1774, by the Lord of Dartmouth to Governor Martin, there is an indication that the Assembly had passed an act pertaining to quit-rents which had been sent over for the King's approval ten years before hostilities broke out between the two countries.[58] The Declaration of Independence, with the accompanying Revolution, ended the discussion of the quit-rent problem upon American soil.

The loose administration of the quit-rent system under the proprietary rule in North Carolina caused much trouble in that territory which might easily have been avoided. In the beginning, the Lords Proprietors' proposal to reserve arbitrarily a half-penny an acre in quit-rents, although many grants in Albemarle had been made by Virginia for half that amount, showed a lack of that nice discernment as to what is suitable, which is necessary for the success of any governmental enterprise. This endeavor to increase the quit-rent rate in Albemarle caused a vigorous remonstrance on the part of the inhabitants until the Lords Proprietors acquiesced, allowing the same rate in this territory as that which existed in Virginia.

---

[56] *The State Records of North Carolina* (Laws), Vol. XXIII, pp. 301–303.

[57] *Colonial Records*, Vol. V, p. 458.

[58] *Ibid.*, Vol. IX, p. 824.

This consent was incorporated in the Great Deed, which later gave rise to many quarrels; the people claimed that it could not be repealed and that it applied to all of North Carolina, while the Lords Proprietors protested against this idea, asserting that they might withdraw the document at their discretion and that in the first place it extended only over the territory of Albemarle.[59] Attempts were made later to raise the rate of quit-rents to a penny per acre, but as the people would not submit to this rule,[60] the usual rates of two shillings per 100 acres remained.

On the whole, the quit-rent system in North Carolina during the proprietary period failed essentially because of the erratic and careless methods of government in existence at that time. One expression of this weakness is to be found in the reduction of rates. Confusion in the land system, rendering impossible the drawing up of a proper rent-roll for collection of quit-rents, was another factor which showed the vacillating character of the proprietary system. The default in collecting quit-rents also had a demoralizing effect upon the local administration, for it was from this source alone that revenue was obtainable for paying the salaries of the chief proprietary officials; the amount collected in quit-rents was, consequently, insufficient to meet the needs. When the Crown purchased Carolina, one of the most urgent needs was a reform in the quit-rent system. Although there was no external change in the governmental administration in Carolina under the royal régime, as distinguished from the proprietary rule, the improvement of the quit-rent system was one of the internal changes attempted.

The Quit-Rent Roll. The device which the Lords Pro-

[59] *Colonial Records,* Vol. I, pp. 175, 176.

[60] *Ibid.,* Vol. I, p. 256. Also the rumor that quit-rents were to be increased helped cause Culpepper's Rebellion.

prietors used to ascertain the amount of aggregate rents from all their lands was called the quit-rent roll. This quit-rent roll contained each landowner's name, the situation of his plot of land, the number of acres in it, and the amount of quit-rents to be paid by him. The first quit-rent roll was formed in 1713 by representatives from the five counties—Chowan, Perquimans, Pasquotank, Currituck, and Bath—who made an enrollment of the lands.[61] Prior to 1713 rents had been collected in a promiscuous fashion without aid of a list, but in that year this list, authorized by the Governor, was submitted to the Lords Proprietors as an index for collecting their rents.

There seems to have been much difficulty in obtaining a satisfactory rent-roll, owing to the growth in the number of settlers, and to the manner in which they received their grants. Although the documents granting the tracts had been signed, many of these regions were neither defined nor surveyed.[62]

Although an act in 1715 forbade the surveying of more than six hundred and forty acres of land in one plot,[63] in 1736 one Henry McCullock was, with some other men, granting lands to the extent of one million and two hundred thousand acres. There were ninety-six grants in this tract consisting of twelve thousand and five hundred acres each.[64] These lands had been obtained for the purpose of securing homes for the religious exiles from France, the French Huguenots, to each of whom was granted a plot of two hundred acres for a homestead.[65] The action of the King in conferring a great part of the

[61] *Colonial Records,* Vol. II, p. 35.

[62] *Ibid.,* Vol. IV, p. 266; Vol. V, p. 95.

[63] *Colonial Records,* Vol. V, p. 94.

[64] *Ibid.,* Vol. V, p. 104.

[65] *Ibid.,* Vol. V, p. 104.

province lands upon Earl Granville did not simplify the
case for quit-rents, as irregular proceedings of this sort
helped to complicate the matter of securing a rent-roll.

In addition to this conglomeration of irregularities concerning the granting of lands and the subsequent accumulation of quit-rents due for collection, the Governors often
complicated matters further by granting lands at prices
which were at variance with those determined by the
Lords Proprietors.   Although, because of this state of
affairs, the Lords Proprietors had ordered the land office
in the colony to be closed in 1715, no great relief had
resulted.[66]   After the close of the office in the colony, land
was supposed to be sold only in London under the supervision of the Lords Proprietors, but there were many violations of this law, notably when the Governor and Council,
in 1724, "gave leave to the people to take up lands in Bath
County requiring a quit-rent of 3 shillings per hundred
acres and cultivation of the land within two years." [67]

A few years later, about the time of the Crown's purchase of Carolina, Sir Richard Everard, then Governor
for the Proprietors, made grants of land to the amount of
400,000 acres, at the rate of £20 for every thousand acres,
upon the pretence of raising money to pay the expense of
running the Boundary Line between North Carolina and
Virginia; the cost of this charge did not amount to more
than £2,000 and, therefore, not more than 100,000
acres should have been granted.   Before the afore-
mentioned grants, it appears that Sir Richard also granted
167,611 acres at 6d per hundred acres; 91,752 acres at
2d per hundred acres; while 30,582 acres of land lapsed
for want of cultivation.   "It appears that patents for the
400,000 acres were issued in a most shameful and im-

[66] *Colonial Records*, Vol. V, p. 95.
[67] *Ibid.*, Vol. V, p. 95.

proper manner being drawn up, signed and sealed in due form, but the persons' names, the number of acres, the descriptions of the Boundary and the sums paid for them, left blank and so issued from the secretary's office just as the clerk or other officer thought proper without any previous survey which was essentially requisite to make the grant valid." "This irregularity gave rise to such endless and exorbitant frauds that it has not been possible at this day [68] to come to any exact knowledge of the state of these grants." [69]

Another factor which added to the difficulty of making a rent-roll was the lack of any established state capital. For many years the Assembly met at various places, such as Edenton, Newbern, and Wilmington, or wherever and whenever the Governor chanced to call a meeting of this body. There was, consequently, no particular place for the records to be kept, and many of them were lost or destroyed in the confusion. Governor Johnston's complaint regarding this condition is found in the following extract from a letter to the Board of Trade in 1748: "The public records lie in a miserable condition, one part of them at Edenton near the Virginia line, in a place without Lock or Key; a great part of them in the Secretary's House at Cape Fear, about Two Hundred Miles Distance from the other, Some few of 'em at the Clerk of the Council's House at Newbern, so that in whatever part of the colony a man happens to be, if he wants to consult any paper or record, he must send some Hundred Miles before he can come at it." [70]

Administration. The quit-rents, which for a number of years were the only taxes levied upon land in the colo-

---

[68] This was written about 1727.
[69] *Colonial Records,* Vol. V, p. 95.
[70] *Ibid.,* Vol. IV, p. 1165.

nies, were not regarded as a source of colonial revenue. They were collected under the supervision of an official appointed by the Lords Proprietors during the ownership of the latter and afterwards by an appointee of the King. This collector was responsible only to these rulers respectively; and was known as the Receiver General. In North Carolina the Receiver General, unlike the one in Virginia, was paid no salary, but received ten per cent of all of the quit-rents which he collected; in addition to this, he was often permitted a fee for the goods or lands which he attached for debts.[71] Not only did the Receiver General collect the quit-rents but he had jurisdiction over their disbursement whenever any amount of them was required for some expenditure within the colony. Orders for such disbursement proceeded from the Lords Proprietors until 1729, and from that date until the Revolution from the King.[72] Since the Governor was the direct representative of the Lords Proprietors or the Crown, the Receiver General made his reports concerning the finances to this executive and his council.[73]

The Receiver General, in his turn, had deputies who made the actual collection from the settlers, each deputy giving a bond of £1,000 as security against any irregularity or fraud for which he might possibly be liable while holding his position. For his efforts the deputy received five per cent of the proceeds;[74] since the Receiver General was allowed ten per cent, at least fifteen per cent of the money collected in quit-rents went to pay for their collection. Once a year each deputy made a report of all

---

[71] *Colonial Records,* Vol. VI, p. 756.

[72] *Ibid.,* Vol. VII, p. 484; *The State Records of North Carolina,* Vol. XI, p. 5.

[73] *Ibid.,* Vol. VII, p. 150.

[74] *Colonial Records,* Vol. V, p. 422.

the land grants, on and off the quit-rent roll, together with the sum collected.[75] As time progressed, however, the sheriffs replaced the deputies as local collectors and received the conventional five per cent reward for their efforts.[76]

In addition to the Receiver General, with his assistants, there was an auditor whose duty it was to keep the accounts of the realm. "His business chiefly consists in auditing the accounts of the Receiver General of the quit-rents and giving debentures for payment of the salaries to the officers upon the Crown's establishment in certifying and entering the warrants for survey of lands granted by the Crown and auditing the patents of these lands, for certifying and auditing of which warrant and patent be both certain fees allowed him." [77] In addition to these duties the auditor was also required to prepare for the Receiver General a quit-rent roll.[78] The Assembly granted fees to the auditor as payment for his services,[79] but the actual work in the colony was performed by a deputy auditor.[80] The Crown also appointed a commissioner "for supervising, inspecting and controlling" the "revenues and grants of land" in the provinces of North and South Carolina, "giving and granting unto him full power to examine and enquire into all frauds, concealments, neglects, delays and abuses with respect to the grants of lands there and the quit-rents payable thereupon." [81]

Fiscal Importance. The Lords Proprietors originally made quit-rents payable in English money but this system

[75] *Colonial Records,* Vol. V, p. 423.

[76] *Ibid.,* Vol. VI, p. 621.

[77] *Ibid.,* Vol. VII, pp. 484, 485.

[78] *Ibid.,* Vol. V, p. 588.

[79] *Ibid.,* Vol. VII, p. 485; Vol. IV, p. 1128.

[80] *Ibid.,* Vol. VII, p. 484.

[81] *The State Records of North Carolina,* Vol. XI, p. 31.

proved impracticable for coined money was very scarce in
the colony at that time.[82]   Since local conditions necessitated a modification in the medium of payment, the people
of Albemarle wished to adopt the Virginia system whereby
the settlers were allowed to pay their quit-rents in tobacco.[83]   This medium of exchange appealed to them as
convenient and as the only type available for the majority,
so they petitioned the Lords Proprietors for permission
to pay their quit-rents in tobacco and a few other commodities, in accordance with the valuation placed upon
these commodities by three or more deputies, designated
by the Governor.[84]   This petition was granted in 1668
by the Lords Proprietors, and the commodities thus classified for the payment of quit-rents were used to general advantage near the coast where the goods could
be easily conveyed to their destination by ships.   As
settlements progressed from the coast toward the
mountains, however, the use of these commodities involved serious drawbacks,—transportation became more
difficult, and it was discovered that there was a wider
range of variability in the quality of commodities than
in that of metal coins.   The settlers took advantage
of their creditors, the Lords Proprietors, and shipped
their lowest grade to them in payment of quit-rents,[85]
thereby causing a decrease in the value of the quit-rents.

During the rule of the Lords Proprietors no uniform
reports showing the collection of quit-rents seem to have
been kept, or at least, there is no connected picture presented by any of the records available.   The only law
concerning the disposal or collection of quit-rents, re-

---

[82] *The State Records of North Carolina*, Vol. I, pp. 91, 164.
[83] *Ibid.*, Vol. IV, p. 109.
[84] *Ibid.*, Vol. I, p. 390.
[85] *Colonial Records*, Vol. IV, p. 921.

corded as passed by the General Assembly during this period was enacted in 1715, "for the better regulation of distresses to be made for levys and quit-rents." [86] It authorized all merchandise or commodities which had been seized for debt, to be appraised by "four substantial freeholders of the County," who were required to swear on oath that they would be impartial judges. These goods were to be held for ten days subject to redemption and, if not redeemed within that period, were to be accepted by the party who caused the distraint to be issued.[87] The amount in arrears was small when North Carolina became a royal province and almost all of the quit-rents were paid in commodities, warehouses having been built by the Lords Proprietors throughout the provinces as places for receiving and storing the goods paid to them for quit-rents.

As the collection of quit-rents had been lax, the King, in 1733, as an inducement for their more efficient collection, had a list of salaries formed, stating that these salaries were to be procured from the quit-rent fund; [88] but not even this offer had any weighty effect in stimulating the collection of quit-rents. From 1729 to 1736, £4,200 of rents in arrears were collected; from 1735 to 1748, according to the report of the Receiver General, a total of £13,356, 17s. 9d. in sterling, or an average of £954 for each year.[89] For the four years from 1741 to 1745, £4,003, 1s. 2d. were collected, an average of £800, 3s. 19 3/5d. per year,[90] and from 1745 through 1748, £1,261, 7s. 1d. or an average of £323,

[86] *The State Records of North Carolina,* Vol. XXIII, pp. 22, 23.
[87] *Colonial Records,* Vol. IV, p. 678.
[88] *Ibid.,* Vol. V, pp. 20, 77, 97.
[89] *Ibid.,* Vol. V, p. 20.
[90] *Ibid.,* Vol. V, p. 101.

6s. 9¼d. per year.[91]   In 1751, between May 14 and
October 5, a sum of £161, 8s. was collected.[92]   During
Governor Johnston's administration until the middle of
the year 1743, there is a record of 1,047,000 acres of
land grants in the state, which, it was estimated, should
have yielded £2,094 of quit-rents, exclusive of those accumulated before the royal period.[93]   From the above data
it appears that there was a decrease, rather than an increase, in the collection of quit-rents after officers' salaries
were made payable from them.   A conspicuous instance
of this deduction is furnished by the case of Governor
Johnston's widow.   There was in 1753 an amount of
£13,000 in sterling, owed to her from quit-rents.[94]   This
plan of collecting and paying salaries from quit-rents being evidently not practical, Governor Dobbs, in 1754,
asked the Board of Trade to influence the King to adopt
other sources for obtaining payment of governmental
expenditures within the colony.[95]

There seem to have been two outstanding reasons for
the enormous decrease in the collection of quit-rents, of
which one was undoubtedly the lack of an adequate quit-
rent roll, while the sale of about half the state to Earl
Granville by the King was the other.   This latter grant
was made in 1744 and included that portion of North
Carolina between thirty-five degrees, thirty-four minutes
and thirty-six degrees, thirty minutes, "north latitude." [96]

During the latter part of Johnston's administration,
Germans and Scotch-Irish began to pour into the state in
large numbers.   Ashe says that "in 1746 Matthew Rowan

[91] *Colonial Records,* Vol. V, pp. 78, 101.

[92] *Ibid.,* Vol. V, p. 21.

[93] *Ibid.,* Vol. IV, p. 1136.

[94] *Ibid.,* Vol. V, p. 22.

[95] *Ibid.,* Vol. V, p. 78.

[96] *Ibid.,* Vol. V, p. 101.

was in the western region, and estimated that there were not above one hundred fighting men in the entire section between Virginia and South Carolina. Seven years later he thought that there were thirty times as many, and said their numbers were increasing daily." [97] This influx of settlers increased the number of landholdings, and, in consequence, the grants of land from which quit-rents were collected, multiplied. In spite of the French and Indian War, about the middle of the eighteenth century, the collection of quit-rents was augmented, the Receiver General's report disclosing a collection, between 1770 and 1772, of £2,242, 7s. 9½d., or an average of £1,121, 5s. 10d. for each year. [98]

Notwithstanding this unquestionable increase in the collection of quit-rents, the officers for the Crown, who were also landowners, were careless in paying their dues; when the time came for them to receive their salaries, however, they were insistent upon obtaining their full share. [99] In 1773, only £996, 6s. were collected in quit-rents, [100] although the sum of £11,388 6s. 3d. due to the officers for salaries, was supposed to be paid out of quit-rents. [101] Such a deficit for salaries, to be paid from the collection of quit-rents was, however, not unusual in North Carolina during the colonial period.

The General Significance. The quit-rent system in North Carolina derived its chief significance from the fact that it was the method by which the Crown maintained its feudal relationship to the colony. Then, too, the results which might be obtained from the use of these dues as a source of royal revenue, the disbursement of

[97] Ashe, S. A., *History of North Carolina,* Vol. I, p. 277.
[98] *Colonial Records,* Vol. IX, p. 650.
[99] *Ibid.,* Vol. IX, p. 646.
[100] *Ibid.,* Vol. IX, p. 609.
[101] *Ibid.,* Vol. II, p. 625.

which should be independent of local regulations, cannot be overlooked. This effort to put into execution the quit-rent laws, regardless of local hostility toward such measures, was merely a reflection of the contest between the "external and internal interests, in which the latter conquered." [102] It has been shown that the enforcement of this feudal due in North Carolina was closely allied to the land system, and that the people in this colony never opposed the principle of a quit-rent levy on their lands, but did strenuously struggle against the amounts and methods of assessment. A study of the quit-rent system also demonstrates the difference between institutions of the North and South at that period. Quit-rents were better established in the South than in the North, owing to several facts. In New England the quit-rent system did not receive the impetus that it did in the South, because the Puritan system of free tenure in Massachusetts exerted a great influence on the land system of the surrounding states. In New York and New Jersey a large part of the lands had been granted by the Dutch without quit-rents and, of course, in those states the British grants reserved quit-rents. Extensive land speculation in this territory, which arose partially as a result of the mixed system of landholdings, made the enforcement of the quit-rents a perplexing task. There were, however, states like Pennsylvania which offered a more favorable opportunity for the development of quit-rents than did those in the South. In North Carolina, as in other southern states, there were homogeneous types of land terms, and since practically all settlements there were made by the English, the land grants were made a part of the English feudal system. The quit-rent system was, therefore, es-

[102] Bond, B. W., *The Quit-Rent System in the American Colonies,* p. 439.

tablished automatically, with both the weakness and the strength of that system clearly indicated.

So far as the quit-rents were concerned, the grants to the proprietors in North Carolina seem to have been a mistake, for the proprietors had not the prestige and executive control needed to enforce the system properly. This defective quit-rent system, although passed on to the Crown later, was never effective, partly because local opposition to the methods of enforcement was so strong that the Crown was unable to bring order out of the chaos; failure was inevitable.

To recapitulate, it may be stated that quit-rents represented one type of feudal institution which was transplanted from English to American soil and which survived for a noticeable length of time. A study of this system also reflects the contrast between the North and the South in social and economic institutions. For many years quit-rents were used as a pretext by landowners pleading for the immunity of land from its share in the burden of taxation. Although for a period this was the only land tax in the colony, it cannot be considered a part of the colonial fiscal system, for it was strictly a feudal due which, according to custom, belonged to the English Crown. It is true that the fund obtained from this source was used to pay the salaries of some of the officials in this territory, but only of those employed by the Crown. While it was not a tax in the true sense of the term, it practically occupied the place of a land tax in the colony, although the revenue obtained from it was of no great fiscal importance. With economic and social expansion and the growth of political power among the settlers, revolutionary ideas invaded every institution, including the quit-rent system, until finally, in 1776, when independence of England was declared, quit-rents ceased to exist in the State of North Carolina.

CHAPTER III

CUSTOMS DUTIES

TYPES and Purposes of Customs Levied in the State. In the historical development of public revenue, indirect taxes usually appeared before direct taxes. In the process of formation of the State of North Carolina, along with the federal dues collected under the nomenclature of quit-rents, indirect taxes in the form of customs duties were levied. Records of customs appear before any instance of a direct tax—such, for instance, as the poll—is to be found among the pages of its statute books or in its numerous records. English customs duties, extending to the colonies, existed before there was any recognition of North Carolina as a political unit. Among her various state laws regulating trade and navigation was the act known as "Old Subsidy," passed in 1660, and imposing a tax on imports and exports. The so-called Enumeration Clause in this act selected, to bear the tax, certain commodities produced in the colonies; among these tobacco and sugar were the two most important products. Three years later, when the Province of Carolina was created and granted to the Lords Proprietors, the tobacco duty automatically applied to this colony. No record of a poll tax, or of any direct tax levied upon the inhabitants of the colony, appeared in their annals until after the first decade of the eighteenth century, but indirect taxes in the form of customs duties imposed by British laws were already in existence before the state was formed.

The method of taxation in any society depends upon its public expenditures which, in their turn, depend upon the type of economics underlying and supporting the fibers of social and political life. The economic life in North Carolina during the colonial period was primitive; from the beginning its people were scattered over a few rural communities on the coast, settlements which, as they gradually grew, merged with each other, forming a border of civilization which was destined to spread westward as population increased and was supplemented from other sources. The climate was mild, and contemporary visitors assure us of the fertility of the soil, the exuberance of vegetation, and the abundance of wild life. In contrast with the preference for small agricultural and pasturage farms in New England and in the Middle Atlantic colonies, the tendency in North Carolina was toward farms of a larger size and plantations of tobacco, rice, and indigo. Owing to the peculiarity of her geographical position, North Carolina, situated between Virginia and South Carolina, grew both types of products on her plantations. Tobacco was grown in the north, as in Virginia, while in the southern portion of the state, rice and indigo were produced, as in South Carolina. Forests, rich in timber and naval stores; fisheries, prolific in their yield of sea food; outposts of hunters and trappers, dispersed throughout the colony; these, together with household manufactures, made the colony practically self-supporting at least until the standard of living began to demand products from abroad.

Aside from those developed in the household, manufactures did not appear in North Carolina until about 1775, and even then were slight. This was due to the facts that labor was expensive and was found to be more productive when applied to agriculture, population was meager, and banking and credit facilities were unknown. Consequently, conditions did not present the complex economic problems we face today. Instead of manufacturing her own raw materials, North Carolina found great advantage in shipping these products to England where the demand was great because of the manufacturing system in existence in that country. England needed these products and therefore encouraged direct shipment to her shores from all the colonies.

It must be borne in mind that the Province of Carolina, and, later, the State of North Carolina, was, until the Revolution of 1776, only a colonial possession of England. The statesmen and politicians who guided its destiny were not men chosen entirely in accordance with democratic principles by the people who settled this territory. The people were not self-governing, as they are reputed to be today; equal suffrage was a condition unheard of or unthought of at that time. It is not, however, to be understood that the people had no voice in the government; on the contrary, the inhabitants played an important part in helping to govern themselves; but they were not always the determining factor in the actual policies which were inaugurated by the political body. As a matter of fact, government in this region was sustained by a joint effort of imperial and provincial control, with, perhaps, the imperial usually predominating.

The enactment of laws and decisions in financial matters, therefore, was inextricably interwoven with the coöperation and struggles of these two factors. Before 1691 the legislature, popularly called the General Assembly, was made up of three factors; the Governor, the Council, and the representatives of the people. After that year, however, the Council was called an Upper House and the people's representatives were styled the House of Commons,[1] in imitation of the English administrative form of government. The Governor never represented the people during the colonial period, although in the proprietary period he was the direct agent of the Lords Proprietors, while in the royal period, he performed this function for the King. Mr. Connor says that "it is important to remember that throughout the colonial period, the Governor was never the representative of the people, but during the proprietary period he represented the Lords Proprietors during the royal period, the King."[2] The Council, subsequently transferred to the Upper House, although authorized by the Lords Proprietors and later by the King, was composed of representatives from both powers. At the opposite end of the scale, counterbalancing the Governor, were the representatives of the people, later known as the House of Commons. This body was the instrument through which both imperial and provincial forces sought to pit their strength in an effort to appropriate for themselves the services of the people and the resources of the land of North Carolina.

Of the three predominating types of revenue drawn from the State of North Carolina, the quit-rent represented solely an imposition on behalf of the imperial interests; the customs duties more clearly reflect a combination of the efforts of the two, while the poll tax was more directly authorized by the people. The customs duties admirably illustrate not only the concurrent, but the clashing and divergent, interests in the general relationship existing between the English and the colonial powers in North Carolina. In England laws were made in regard

[1] Connor, R. D. W., *History of North Carolina,* p. 43.
[2] *Ibid.,* p. 40.

to trade and navigation which extended to her various colonial possessions. The Navigation Act of 1660, the Staple Act of 1663, and the Plantation Duties of 1673, were the three acts passed by Parliament which formed the basis for the imposition of English customs duties in the American Colonies.[3] These have been described in a previous chapter. They clearly represent the fact that customs laws, applying to North Carolina and passed on the other side of the ocean, were principally for political purposes, in order to regulate trade and navigation for the furtherance of England's supremacy among the other nations of Europe. Economic life forms the basis for the structure of all other phases of life; power consists in command over services, and power has its roots in economic life. England, recognizing this fact, hastened to lay the foundation for a political empire through her economic activities by commanding the services and cooperation of her colonies. The channel through which these services flowed was via the customs duties; namely, taxes on exchange and transportation. This was the earliest form of taxation represented in North Carolina.

The revenue from this type of customs tax levied in North Carolina always belonged to the English King. The fact should be constantly kept in mind that, during the rule of the Lords Proprietors, as well as during the later period under the royal prerogative, the proceeds from this source were the property of the Crown. Royal officials, appointed by the Sovereign, supervised and collected this tax. The Crown, however, through a spirit of liberality which had as its underlying motive a hope of greater future reward in building up a powerful economic unit in the colonies, often allowed the revenue from the customs to remain in North Carolina to defray the ex-

[3] Beer, G. L., *The Old Colonial System*, Part I, Vol. I, p. 84.

penses of the local government. As the colony grew and its wants became more complex, the expenditures for governmental purposes naturally increased. There was need for more revenue, a need often made acute by wars. How was more revenue to be gained? Because of its slave property, the landed aristocracy, which had the most potent hand in the guidance of the affairs of the state during the early colonial period, was opposed to direct taxation. This opposition was a natural one, for any direct tax at that time would have fallen on accumulated property, and property owners would have borne the entire burden of the tax. This class managed to suppress any tax of this sort until the second decade of the eighteenth century, and indirect taxation continued to predominate in the colony in proportion to the relative strength of the landowning aristocracy over the non-landowning class of freemen. It was thought that by placing an indirect tax on a few articles of exports and imports the tax would be scattered throughout the colony and would fall upon the poorer classes. That this idea was an erroneous one has already been pointed out in Chapter I.

The result, then, of these increasing needs of the state was the levying by the General Assembly of additional customs duties, which usually took the form of import duties on liquors. This type of customs levied by the Assembly was for the purpose of revenue only, as distinguished from the type which England levied in conformity with her trade and navigation policy. It is obvious, therefore, that there were two distinct types of customs duties levied in North Carolina during the colonial era. The first was represented by those customs levied in England on the imports and exports of the colony, such as tobacco, and imposed primarily as regulative measures for trade and navigation; the second, by the customs imposed by the Assembly primarily for the purpose of obtaining revenue for state expenditures. The first type was levied for political purposes, while the second type was imposed for fiscal reasons. Some of the customs placed on the importation of liquors exemplify this latter type. At this point, the fact might be mentioned that in a few instances the General Assembly of North Carolina, for the purpose of conserving the supply within the colony, placed customs duties on articles exported from the colony. As an instance of this, a tax was placed on hides with the intention of preventing a rapid diminution of the supply of live stock in the colony.

All customs duties are classified as either export duties or import duties. In North Carolina the chief levies in the first group were placed on tobacco and hides; in the second group on liquors and tonnage. In following the history of these customs, the principles discussed above should be kept in mind.

The system of customs in North Carolina, which was under the authority of the Southern Treasurer,[4] was administered by officials appointed by the Crown. At the head of the customs department in the state was placed a Surveyor General of the Customs, whose duty it was to see that the customs were enforced. For each port, there was a collector of customs, who, with the assistance of a few deputies, was to be responsible for the actual collection of these duties.

The History of the Export Tax on Tobacco. Since the majority of settlers in Albemarle had migrated from Virginia where the tobacco crops furnished the principal

---

[4] The territory covered by the English Colonies along the Atlantic coast was divided into halves with a Treasurer for the Northern part and a Treasurer for the Southern part who represented the financial interests of England.

means of subsistence, it was not surprising that these people should continue to plant tobacco in their new territory. The growing of tobacco, then, became the chief source of livelihood among the young colonists.

The irregularities of the coast of North Carolina, apparently making for excellent harbors, proved, in reality, only a mirage in which many strange ships were sunk. Numerous sand bars, lurking just beneath the water's surface, infested this coast, forming a menace to large vessels engaged in ocean-going traffic, but as this danger was soon realized the large ships avoided these inlets. As a result of this physical characteristic, tobacco was transported in small ships to Virginia and to New England,[5] and it was not long before thrifty New England traders were a predominating factor in controlling practically all commerce with North Carolina.

For the first seven years no customs were collected in North Carolina, the first charter to the Lords Proprietors having specified this exemption. Although trade was not restricted by any artificial means, the Albemarle colony was automatically subjected after 1670 to the English customs laws. By the Act of 1673, or the so-called Second Navigation Act, England placed a duty of one penny per pound on tobacco, shipped from one colony to another. This commodity was at that time the only one produced in Carolina that could be used for exports. The first tax on tobacco in Virginia, originated after the middle of the seventeenth century, and about a decade before the Lords Proprietors were granted Carolina, had as its objective other purposes than the raising of revenue. The three purposes given for the imposition of this first tax on tobacco in Virginia were: the payment of officers' salaries; the introduction of tobacco as a medium of exchange, and the

[5] *Colonial Records,* Vol. I, pp. 242-244.

encouragement of a diversification of products.[6] In producing a single commodity there was always danger of famine and misery whenever a shortage or failure in that one product occurred. It was not until the sixties that tobacco was taxed for revenue in Virginia, while in Carolina, although revenue considerations were partly responsible for the export tax on tobacco, the fundamental reason during the seventeenth century was political rather than fiscal. In England's general colonial policy, export duties on tobacco in this colony were subordinate. The merchants in North Carolina had a choice of two methods of procedure in paying duties on exports: they might pay them to the customs officials at the ports when shipments were ready to be sent out, or they might give a bond to insure payment at the other end,—that is, when the ship reached its destination in an English port.

Until 1676 the Lords Proprietors seem to have been busy with other affairs at home to the neglect of the Albemarle community. About that time, however, their attention was attracted to the excessive and almost exclusive trade which had been developed between this province and New England. Clearly, New England was seducing from Albemarle the tobacco exports which should have been sent directly to England. Although this was a violation of Great Britain's Navigation Acts, Carolina was continuing her trade without any effective force being used to prohibit this smuggling. In this year the Lords Proprietors directed the Governor and Council to use all means at their disposal for drawing this tobacco trade to England, claiming that impoverishment to the North Carolina settlers would be unavoidable "if they buy goods at 2d hand" and sell these commodities at a lower rate

---

[6] Hening, W. W., *Virginia: Laws, Statutes*, Vol. I, p. 410; Ripley, W. Z., *The Financial History of Virginia*, pp. 507–508.

than prices in England.[7]   In these instructions there was
another paragraph which made mandatory an accurate
report of the topographical peculiarities of the coast of
Albemarle, with emphasis upon the shallowness or depth
of water in the sounds and bays where ships might land
for the purpose of taking on or disposing of a cargo.
The Lords Proprietors claimed that hitherto these facts
had been "so concealed and uncertainly reported" to them
in England that they had become suspicious that some
persons among the settlers had joined with the New Eng-
landers in engrossing Albemarle's "poor trade," thus keeping the people of this region under the domination of
New England.[8]

In the decade between 1670 and 1680 the tobacco crop
of North Carolina has been estimated to have yielded
about two thousand hogsheads.[9]   Since a hogshead was
approximately five hundred pounds of tobacco, it follows
that about one million pounds of tobacco was exported
from North Carolina during this period.   Some of this
was shipped to England, but the greater portion of it
seems to have been sent to other colonies.   Upon the
portion sent to the other colonies a duty of one penny a
pound was imposed by the Act which Parliament had
passed in 1673.   Had this duty been collected, it would
have effectively diverted the tobacco trade to England; but
the directions of this law were not followed in practice,
and the attempt at enforcement resulted in such a revolt
in Albemarle, with New England traders secretly applaud-
ing the rebels, that efforts to apply it were eventually
abandoned.

The trouble started in 1675.   In that year Governor

[7] *Colonial Records,* Vol. I, pp. 230–232.
[8] *Ibid.,* Vol. I, pp. 230–232; see also pp. 247, 265, 266.
[9] Beer, G. L., *The Old Colonial System,* Part I, Vol. II, p. 195.

Jenkins of Albemarle received commissions for the official installation of Copley as Collector of Customs and Birch as Comptroller. If these men should happen not to be in the colony at the time, the Governor was authorized to fill the vacancies with his own selection. Since the enforcement of the one penny duty on tobacco accompanied these orders, the officials were confronted with strenuous opposition, engendered largely by the fear in the minds of the Albemarle producers that the New England traders would increase the price of their merchandise. With the prospect of a considerable rise in prices of commodities which they needed for their own consumption, the people of the North Carolina colony became mutinous, abusing and threatening the members of the Council. The Governor and his staff contrived to allay the indignation of the people and appointed Timothy Biggs, one of Earl Craven's deputies, as surveyor of customs, and Valentine Byrd, as collector of customs. These men for a brief time gave the impression of attempting to collect the duties, but they were lax in performing their functions. The law, nevertheless, furnished a source of continual friction.

There was about this time, a general spread of discontent throughout the colony. Reports were circulated among the people that the entire province of Carolina was to be divided among the Lords Proprietors and that Albemarle was to be assigned to Sir William Berkeley— that tyrant of Virginia. This idea was naturally obnoxious to the liberty-loving inhabitants of Albemarle. Accompanying this report was another one threatening an increase in quit-rents. This latter rumor almost caused an insurrection; but the Assembly, which met in November, 1675, expostulated with the Lords Proprietors on these topics and the revolt was deferred.

Combined with these difficulties was a war with the Indians. A fierce tribe of Indians fell upon the Meherrins in southern Virginia and started trouble. They prowled through the country bordering on Albemarle and aroused the wrath of the settlers by committing a number of atrocious murders. Although Albemarle colony organized and took up arms against the Indians, the war lasted until 1677 when the Indians were ejected from Carolina. During this war, in the year 1676, when the fighting abated because the people were equipped with arms, the colonists decided to force the Governor to make concessions respecting the tobacco tax.[10] They requested cancellation of the tax on tobacco exported to another colony, and threatened revolt. The ground of complaint lay not against the proprietors and their government, but against the English laws. One of the methods which England followed in order to build up a great empire was to require the colonies to trade directly and exclusively with her merchants in London, and to forbid intercolonial traffic in tobacco. The people of Albemarle were allowed to ship tobacco directly to England without any duty on this export, but a tax was placed on that shipped to New England or to any other colony. This caused the value of tobacco to decrease by the amount of the tax—that is, one penny on the pound in this case. New England had the supplies which Albemarle wanted, and it was easier of access than England, and nearer; but as England considered this trade useful to London, it was prohibited.

Everybody works for his own interests, and naturally the people in Albemarle wished to gain the greatest advantage from their trade. In this particular instance,

---

[10] *Colonial Records,* Vol. I, pp. 291-293.

England's immediate interest seems to have been opposed to that of Albemarle; at least, Albemarle held views which were not in harmony with English opinion on the subject under discussion. The inhabitants of Albemarle reasoned in this manner: they had not made this offensive law; they had received no advantage as a result of its execution; they had suffered a decrease in the value of their product because of it; and they were exposed to many inconveniences on account of it. Since England had imposed it to benefit her own merchants, the inhabitants of Albemarle did not yield placidly. The result was discord, the usual consequence of misunderstanding, and a failure to take into consideration any viewpoint other than the one of selfish interest. Both parties in this case obeyed this impulse, a natural one, to be sure, because the human mind is usually incapable of grasping more than one view at a time.

At first, before they felt capable of successful open combat, the people evaded the law by various ingenious devices. Many hogsheads of tobacco, smuggled from Albemarle to New England, were carried to Boston and reshipped under the name of fish to foreign countries. As a result New England had a monopoly of Albemarle's tobacco trade. Later, people took up arms openly against the law requiring high export duties on tobacco.[11] George Durant, a wealthy and influential citizen of Albemarle, who shipped a great quantity of tobacco to New England, was one of the leaders of this rebel party which numbered Valentine Byrd among its members. The few officials of the administration, not being able to suppress the community uprising, made a compromise, and, though no authority had been given them by the Crown, they offered

---

[11] *Colonial Records,* Vol. I, p. 245.

to reduce the tobacco tax to one farthing per pound. This offer was accepted and affairs probably would have remained quiet for a while had not personal prejudices and political intrigues continued to keep the colony in disorder, causing the Lords Proprietors to attempt stern measures in the solution of the problem.

As conditions in the colony were in disorder, the proprietors decided to substitute a new Governor to manage affairs, in the mistaken idea that these difficulties could be solved by administrative measures. No remedy is ever ultimately effective unless it strikes at the source from which the trouble springs, which in this particular difficulty was to be found in the trade laws enacted by the English Parliament. Thomas Eastchurch, who was selected to act as Governor for the colony, was sent from England with directions to restrain the trade between Albemarle and New England, and Thomas Miller was sent with him to perform the duties of Collector of Customs. En route to Carolina, Eastchurch, being detained by personal matters in the West Indies, sent Miller ahead to govern the colony until he should arrive. Miller as Governor attempted to force many harsh measures upon the people. As Collector of Customs he maintained the same attitude [12] and, through the aid of his deputies, vigorously enforced the English trade laws. As a result of these measures, many hogsheads of tobacco were seized, along with commodities from Europe which had been smuggled into the colony.[13] The enforcement of these laws curtailed trade with New England to a great extent; the people of Albemarle became inflamed with anger, and conflict was inevitable.

The rebellion started during the latter part of 1677.

[12] *Colonial Records,* Vol. I, pp. 278–284, 286–289, 326–328.
[13] *Ibid.,* Vol. I, pp. 255, 264–267.

An indication of its cause is furnished by the leaders of the insurrection. Among the chief agitators were Captain Valentine Byrd,[14] the previous Collector of Customs, a man of considerable wealth, who had allowed tobacco to be exported to New England without bringing pressure to bear upon the collection of the exports due; Captain Zachariah Gillam, a prominent Albemarle trader; John Culpepper, a renegade from South Carolina; and the traders of New England who had been profiting by the illicit trade.[15] Of these, Culpepper was the most conspicuous figure; in fact, this revolt was known as "Culpepper's Rebellion." He led the attack against the existing government; Miller was consigned to prison, and the goods which Miller had confiscated and the duties which he had collected in demanding obedience to the law were also seized by this rebellious body. Culpepper was appointed Governor, was made Collector of Customs, and ruled the subjects of the land for almost two years. In 1678 Timothy Biggs was appointed by the Crown to be Comptroller and Surveyor of Customs in Albemarle, but Culpepper, having appropriated this position, denied the office to Biggs and continued to exercise the privilege for himself.[16]

The proprietors, hearing of this uprising, decided to send one from among their ranks to take charge of the situation, and the choice fell on Seth Sothel for this mission. Since Miller was awaiting trial for his actions, the Commissioners of the Customs in England, designated Sothel to act as Collector in Albemarle. Sothel, however, had the misfortune to be captured by pirates on the journey to the colony, and three Governors were des-

---

[14] *Colonial Records,* Vol. I, pp. 256, 257, 265, 266.
[15] *Ibid.,* Vol. I, pp. 286–289.
[16] *Ibid.,* Vol. I, pp. 246, 275–277.

tined to manage the affairs of this unhappy colony before Sothel was released. In the meantime, Robert Holden was appointed Collector of Customs to act in Sothel's place. Holden and Timothy Biggs, the Royal Comptroller of the Customs, had a violent dispute, but by 1680 the turmoil had ceased and peace was established in the colony. This was brought about by conciliatory measures which the Lords Proprietors were wise enough to offer. Since some of the leaders of the revolution had been dispersed, while others had become reconciled, the inhabitants of Albemarle "quietly paid" his Majesty's customs.[17] In addition to this, the colony acquiesced in a law passed by the Assembly imposing a tax upon the people for the purpose of repaying the money and goods appropriated by them during the revolution.[18]

The Crown had threatened to invalidate the Lords Proprietors' charter to Carolina unless they could enforce order within the colony. The Lords Proprietors were chiefly concerned with their desire to keep their charter, and, consequently, in representing conditions in the colony to the Crown, minimized the seriousness of their predicament. The reputation of Albemarle, a primitive community composed of people whom no power could dominate for long in opposition to the will of the people, was generally unfavorable. During the decade subsequent to the Culpepper Rebellion, there was scarcely any attempt on the part of its owners to regulate the affairs of the colony; although quiet seems to have prevailed, the records of the occurrences during this time are inadequate for further deductions.

Some writers have estimated the number of people living in Albemarle about 1682 as between 2,000 and 3,000,

[17] *Colonial Records*, Vol. I, pp. 286–289, 318–321, 326–328.
[18] *Ibid.*, Vol. I.

a larger population than that of the settlement around Charles Town in South Carolina. While the chief produce was tobacco, a small amount of beef and pork was exported to the West Indies. Direct trade with England was inconsiderable, so that in 1679, when Virginia refused to allow Carolina to ship tobacco into her territory, the main volume of tobacco was directed to New England. This export to New England continued until the Revolution in 1776. The only collection districts for exports and imports in Carolina during the seventeenth century were Currituck and Roanoke. Currituck had no fixed place for entry, but Roanoke had Edenton for its port. In 1715, with the growth and scattering of population, exports and imports had increased to such an extent that another port was needed. Bath, on the Pamlico Sound, was accordingly made a port of entry, and in 1722, Beaufort, at Topsoil Inlet, was added to the number of ports of entry. Before the middle of the eighteenth century there were five ports of entry in North Carolina, for Brunswick, on Cape Fear River, had been added. This increase of ports of entry would indicate a growing trade and in consequence a larger amount of duties on the exports and imports accruing to the government, whether collected or not.

During the eighteenth century the New England trade continued, and, as the English navigation and trade laws were still on the statute books, the one penny per pound tax on tobacco shipped from one colony to another remained incorporated in the law. There is, however, no proof or even any indication that the law was enforced; on the contrary, the evidence supports the opposite view. In the first place, indications of fraud corroborate this opinion. Throughout the colonial era, there is proof in the records and communications of the entire period of over a hundred years that fraud was prolific. There were numerous instances in the laws and in letters to England indicative of the existence of such a state of affairs, laws which attempted to repress the fraud; letters which complained of it. These furnished one indubitable proof that the export tax on tobacco was not collected. In the second place, the enforcement of a tax of one penny a pound on exports of tobacco to New England would have been oppressive to Albemarle. It would have been a burden too heavy to bear, for trade would have been reduced, and as their wants remained unsatisfied, the people would have suffered in a corresponding degree.

Moreover, in the third place, had the tax been collected on the approximately one million pounds of tobacco which the country raised for exportation, in the seventies, for instance, England would have received about £4,000 in revenue. Since no amount remotely resembling this can be traced in the customs receipts, it is reasonably safe to assume that the total sum accruing from this tax was never collected. Considering the tumult raging in the colony on this question during the latter part of the seventeenth century, the correct inference seems to be that the customs officials were incapable of executing the law because of the general opposition to it. There are, however, no records available showing the revenue obtained from export duties on tobacco in North Carolina.

During the eighteenth century, the output of tobacco tended to decrease. Although the rate of duty remained constant, we have every reason to believe that a more than proportionate decrease in customs from North Carolina resulted. This, as we have seen, was due to various reasons, chief of which was the opportunity for "smuggling offered by the North Carolina coast and sounds." [19]   Accounts

[19] *Colonial Records,* Vol. III, p. XVI.

written about the middle of the eighteenth century indicate that great quantities of North Carolina tobacco were
exported through the New England skippers without duty.
These skippers were the chief smugglers, but Virginia and
North Carolina were beneficiaries and also participants
in the traffic; the Crown was thus defrauded of revenue
to which it was entitled. England, nevertheless, continued
to collect from North Carolina, on exports of tobacco, a
small amount of revenue, which it usually devoted to the
payment of officers' salaries and fees in the state. At no
time did this duty play any very important part in the
state's revenues, as it did, for instance, in Virginia. In
fact, in the eighteenth century not much importance was
attached to this duty and when hostilities started between
the two commonwealths in 1776, it automatically ceased.

Import Duties on Liquors. The charter given to the
Lords Proprietors in 1663 granted an exemption of seven
years from customs duties in Carolina. According to
another provision in this document, after the expiration
of the seven years, the eight proprietors "their heirs and assigns, may from time to time forever, have and enjoy, the
customs and subsidies in the ports, harbours, creeks, and
other places within the province aforesaid, payable for
goods, merchandise, and wares, there laded or to be laded,
or unladed, the said customs to be reasonably assessed,
upon any occasion, by themselves, and by and with the
consent of the free people there, or the greater part of
them aforesaid; to whom we give power by these presents, for us, our heirs and successors, upon just cause and
in due proportion, to assess and impose the same." [20] The
Lord Proprietors and the Assembly thus enjoyed the
privilege of imposing taxes on certain articles imported
or exported from the colony for purposes of revenue.

[20] *Colonial Records,* Vol. I, p. 28.

During the seventeenth century, North Carolina and South Carolina were both under the rule of one Governor. Albemarle, at that time, was the only section settled in North Carolina, but by the beginning of the eighteenth century the number of inhabitants of Albemarle had begun to increase. From the time of North Carolina's separation from South Carolina, until the Crown bought North Carolina in 1729, the population of the latter had increased from less than 8,000 to over 36,000 inhabitants. About the third decade of the eighteenth century there were a few scattered colonists along the coast, but these were insignificant as a political unit. In 1711 there occurred an atrocious massacre of some of these scattered colonists on the Neuse River and Pamlico, instigated principally by the Tuscarora Indians. Prior to this, there had been the Cary Rebellion in Virginia in which North Carolina demanded more attention than had been given to it previously by the Lords Proprietors. On the twenty-fourth of January, 1712, the Lords Proprietors issued a commission for the appointment of Hyde, as first Governor of North Carolina now separate and distinct from South Carolina.[21] He received his appointment on May 7, 1712, and from that date this colony had its individual Governor to supervise and direct its government.

From the records it appears that no import duty on liquors was levied in Albemarle until it became a distinct political unit. At that time governmental expenses naturally increased; the war against the Tuscaroras made the expenses of government very heavy, and duties were laid on both exports and imports to meet these expenditures. In 1712 an issue of £4,000 of paper currency was authorized by the legislature, "the first of such currency issued

---

[21] *Colonial Records*, Vol. I, p. xxxi.

by the colony." [22]   The Tuscarora War dragged on until
1718, although the power of the majority of the Indian
tribes was broken and treaties had been signed in 1715.
The population in 1716 all told, young and old, men and
women, black and white, was estimated to be only about
8,000.   In November, 1717, Mr. Urmstone proposed to
the Secretary methods of taxation for meeting the public
debt incurred as a result of the war; this debt, which
amounted to £16,000 had been floated in public bills of
credit.   For the withdrawal of these bills Urmstone estimated that £9,000 could be collected from polls, while
£6,000 might be obtained from a land tax; "and for raising the other 1,000 pounds," he continues, "a duty might
be laid on all strong liquors imported from anywhere *but
the West Indies* which in three years might easily raise
the other 1,000 pounds, to balance and clear all the county
debts." [23]   In addition to the proposal for the imposition
of this duty, there was a hint at regulation of imports of
liquors for public welfare in the following lines: "And it
is very evident that the importing so much strong liquor
into the country greatly impovereth the people." [24]   The
idea, however, of regulating the supply of liquor to the
colonies seems never to have been considered by the statesmen during this period; the liquor duty was imposed for
revenue only.

Governor Eden, who had become Governor in 1714
and had steered the colony towards prosperity and peace
after the Indian war, died in March, 1722.   It was not
until about two years later that Burrington arrived to take
the oath of office, the affairs of state having been managed
meanwhile by the Assembly.   Among the annals of this

[22] *Colonial Records,* Vol. I, pp. 837–839.
[23] *Ibid.,* Vol. II, p. 296.
[24] *Ibid.,* Vol. II.

period appears a law, passed by Parliament, relating to customs in England to be carried out by Burrington upon arriving in North Carolina. This was "An Act for laying further duties upon sweets and for lessening the duties as well upon vinegar as upon certain low wines and whale Tins and the duties upon Brandy imported." [25] This would indicate the existence of a duty on liquor but it is supported by no further evidence.

During the reign of the Lords Proprietors, therefore, import duties on liquors to the colony in North Carolina seem to have been negligible, or perhaps non-existent. Until the Crown bought this territory in 1729, the poll tax seemed to have been the chief source of revenue. The poorer inhabitants, upon whom the burden of this tax principally fell, began to exercise more voice in the government and to murmur against the polls. Population had been steadily increasing, and in 1733 Governor Burrington reported 30,000 whites, 6,000 negroes, and 800 Indians, making a total of 36,800 in all. Although North Carolina never had as large a number of wealthy slave owners as Virginia, she nevertheless had a sufficient number, in relation to the rest of her population, to hold the balance of power in political life. This wealthy class transplanted to the colony the so-called more refined standards of living of the old world. North Carolina was a wilderness; it required more than a highly cultured class of people to subdue her. Naturally, as the population grew, it was influenced by its surroundings; the hardy stock survived and flourished; while the more protected element was slow in developing. Consequently, as the non-landowning classes developed in numbers and in political power, they began to oppose a poll tax. The

[25] Clarke's *Laws of North Carolina*.

landed class, seeking to quiet the poorer classes, and yet, at the same time, attempting themselves to evade the tax burden as far as possible, decided to put a tax on commodities. As a result of this step, the General Assembly, at a meeting in 1734, passed the following bill for a tax on liquors imported to the colony: "An Act for laying a Duty on Liquors, for and toward defraying the contingent charges of government; and to make a poll-tax on the poorer inhabitants more easy." [26] The rate of this tax is not known, for only the title to the bill remains.

For more than a decade thereafter, there is no record of a duty on liquors, but when the legislature met in March, 1747, it authorized a commission to revise and print the laws of the province. Together with a duty on rice, a duty was placed on wine, rum and distilled liquors imported into the province. There was imposed upon every gallon of these liquors that should be imported into the government "from any port of place (Great Britain excepted) either by Land or water, the Duty of three pence proclamation money or Bills equivalent, or the value thereof in the same liquor" for which the duty was payable.[27] In the October session of 1748 the Assembly amended the act of a former year by a law entitled, "An Act for appointing commissioners to revise and print the Laws of this Province; and for granting unto his Majesty for defraying the charge thereof, a Duty on Wine, Rum, and distilled liquors and rice, imported into this province.[28] In 1749, an act was passed confirming the revision of the laws and the contingent duties. When, in 1752, more money was needed for defraying governmental expenses, along with other taxes a duty of fourpence

[26] Clarke's *Laws of North Carolina.*
[27] *Ibid.,*
[28] *The State Records of North Carolina,* Vol. XXIII, p. 308.

(proclamation money) per gallon was placed on light wines for a period of three years, this rise of one penny in the rates continued for a few years, for in 1754 the duty of fourpence per gallon on wines imported was extended for three years. The French and Indian War had started and as more money was needed to carry on the war, the Assembly in 1756 levied an additional duty of twopence per gallon for a period of one year upon all wines, rum and other spirituous liquors to be imported into the province. This duty, with a poll tax, was levied upon the inhabitants for granting £3,400 as aid to His Majesty to erect a fort and pay two companies of soldiers for the defense of the western frontier of the province. Two years later, in the April Session of the Legislature of 1758, as the war was still being waged, the poll tax was increased, and an additional tax of twopence per gallon was placed on all wines and distilled liquors imported into the province for the next four years. This tax was imposed for granting aid to the Crown to pay troops "joined under command of Brigadier-General Forbes," and for placing garrisons in forts and on the coast.

In 1764 the Governor, in his speech to the Assembly urging the taxation of certain imports and exports for "necessities of government," advocated raising revenue from "Luxuries by adding a duty upon wine, spirits and other fermented liquors imported (except from Great Britain) and upon all brought in by Land from the adjoining colonies." [29] There is one instance in 1767 where a duty of one penny per gallon was placed on imported liquors for the benefit of a school. A letter from Mr. Reed to the Secretary in 1772 contains this interesting

[29] *Colonial Records,* Vol. VI, p. 1218.

passage about a duty for the maintenance of Mr. Tomlinson's Academy: "You may see by the Act of Assembly for establishing the school, which I sent you the 23rd of January, 1767, that one penny per gallon, for a limited time, is laid upon all spirituous Liquors imported into Neuse River, for the Benefit of the School; out of which twenty pounds p ann: is to be paid to the School-master, to enable him to keep an assistant and the rest is to be applied to the education of poor children, not exceeding Ten." [30]   The regular import duty on liquors at this time was sixpence per gallon, which made the tax on wines sevenpence. Governor Tryon confirmed this fact in a letter to the Earl of Shelbourne in 1767, stating that "the county duties laid upon wines and spirituous liquors imported into the several ports of this province are sixpence per gallon and one penny extraordinary duty on the imports into Neuse River for the purpose of the support of the school at Newbern." [31]

There seem to have been no periodic statements of the income to the state from this import tax on liquor, and, although the revenue obtained from the tax was not an amount to be despised inasmuch as it was used to a considerable extent in financing wars, there is no record indicating that it was as certain and as productive as the poll tax. The unproductivity of the liquor tax was obviously due in large measure to the great amount of smuggling which went on in North Carolina; since, although the people consumed large quantities of liquor, thus demanding a considerable importation into the colony, no large amount of revenue was collected for the simple reason that the peculiarities of the coast formation invited a great deal of smuggling. The rates on liquors were as high as seven-

[30] *Colonial Records,* Vol. IX, p. 239.
[31] Ashe, A. S., *History of North Carolina,* Vol. I.

pence per gallon for a time after 1767 and as low as three-pence in 1747, twenty years before; the usual rate was about sixpence. The careless method of administration of the laws and the rigorous penalties imposed for evasion of these duties indicate the prevalence of much fraud. Although Virginia had found a duty of about threepence most successful in the production of revenue, the rate in North Carolina averaged about twice that amount; it is not difficult, therefore, to understand the reason for the evasion of so many of these duties. It must ever be kept in mind, however, that these duties were never relied upon as the chief source of revenue in North Carolina; they were always used as a supplement to other taxes for defraying some specific governmental expense.

Import Duties on Rice. In addition to the import duties on liquors in the laws of 1748 and 1749, a duty was levied on rice which was to bear the same import tax during this brief period. This duty was imposed at this time for the purpose of defraying the expenses connected with the revision of the laws of the province. No further mention of a duty on rice occurs in the annals of North Carolina.

Tonnage Duties. In 1722 population had spread over a wider area, and people were settling in Craven and along the Neuse and Roanoke rivers.[32] During this year Governor Eden died, after having conducted the affairs of the colony in a peaceful manner for several years. About this time a new precinct called Carteret was established by the council; Beaufort was incorporated and made a port for the collection of customs, and a road was established between Core Point and Newbern. The growth of the province had been obstructed by lack of commercial facilities, so, in order to hasten improvements in this

[32] Ashe, S. A., *History of North Carolina*, Vol. I, p. 206.

phase of economic life, a settlement was encouraged at Ocracoke Inlet where there was a favorable harbor.[33] Lighthouses were needed and improvements on the harbor were essential to the establishment and upkeep of this port. What could be more natural than to levy a tax on incoming vessels for the maintenance of the port? Accordingly, in 1723, the Assembly passed "An Act for appropriating part of the Impost Duty on Vessels, or Powder Money, to Beacon out the Channels from Roanoke to Ocracork Inlets, and several other things to facilitate the Trade and Navigation of this government." [34] This tonnage duty on vessels continued at intervals, as occasion demanded.

In 1754 another act was passed granting to His Majesty, for a period of two years, "A Duty on the tonnage of ships and other vessels coming into the province." [35] The rate was a half pound of gun powder and one pound of shot of lead for every ton of the ship. This act was amended in 1756 and the rate was fixed at two shillings per ton instead of payment in powder and lead. In 1762 there was enacted, for five years, "An Act to amend and further continue an Act, entitled, An Act for facilitating the Navigation of Port Bath, Port Roanoke, & Port Beauford; passed the 31 day of May, 1752." [36] In this act the rates on vessels were progressive: on vessels with a 5 ton burden, a tax of six shillings was placed; on those above 50 tons or under 100 tons, the tax was twelve shillings; on those above 100 tons, the tax was twenty shillings.

There was, then, no customary rate which was stable

---

[33] Ashe, S. A., *History of North Carolina*, Vol. I, p. 207.
[34] Clarke's *Laws of North Carolina*.
[35] *Ibid.*
[36] *Ibid.*

over a long period of time; each rate was special and applied to specific ports. The tonnage duty was a minor one, of slight importance in the colonial taxation system of North Carolina; it disappeared entirely with the Revolution and with the passage of the other feudal institutions from American soil.

Export Tax upon Hides. In addition to the export taxes on tobacco levied for political reasons, and the import duties on liquors and vessels, levied for revenue, there was an export tax sometimes levied on hides in Carolina for sumptuary purposes. These three duties cover the entire range of indirect taxes levied in North Carolina.

In 1748 an act was passed for preventing the exportation of "Raw Hides, Pieces of Hides, & Calf-skins" out of North Carolina.[87] Ten shillings in proclamation money was required to be paid over to government officials for each piece of hide which was received on board, and should a collector clear a vessel without administering the oath, declaring no hides, he was penalized by a fine of fifty pounds. This act remained in force for fifteen years. The prohibitive rate placed upon hides was principally for the purpose of conserving the supply of leather for home consumption, as the revenue collected from this source was very small, and was given to the churches in some of the localities from which it was collected.

The chief significance of the export tax on hides was the fact that this was the only product of North Carolina, except tobacco, which was taxed on its exportation. Tobacco was taxed by the English Government for political reasons, while hides were taxed by the colony for sumptuary reasons. The revenue derived by the state from customs sources was principally on the import of liquors

[87] Clarke's *Laws of North Carolina.*

and, in one instance, of rice. Although import duties on liquors brought the state no inconsiderable revenue, they were difficult to collect and subject to easy evasion. It remained for the poll tax to bear the chief burden of financing governmental expenditures in North Carolina during the colonial era.

CHAPTER IV

THE POLL TAX

ADVENT of Direct Taxation. The indirect form of taxation, illustrated by the duties on imports and exports previously reviewed, had been in operation in Carolina for half a century before the direct tax was used to any appreciable extent. There is a statement vaguely indicating the probable use of a poll tax during this early period, but there is no concrete evidence in support of it.[1] The last poll tax levied in England was in 1698, and, although this form of tax was never very popular with the English, it is possible that the members of the Albemarle colony might have attempted about this time a mild imitation of their English cousins.[2] In this primitive society, indirect taxes had been sufficient to meet the few governmental expenses necessary for the maintenance of the colony as a political body, but as the colony grew, the necessity for greater income for the upkeep of the government presented itself; an additional source of revenue was needed. About the middle of the second decade in the eighteenth century, the people of the colony had succeeded in subduing the Indians in the territory, but war debts were impending. The desolation following the close of the Tuscarora War, however, had not been en-

---

[1] *Colonial Records,* Vol. II, Prefatory notes, p. v.
[2] Palgrave's *Dictionary of Political Economy;* Dowell's *History of Taxation and Taxes in England,* pp. 15-63.

tirely without a counter-balance. As fear of the Indians
abated, immigration from other states began, plantations
started to multiply, stretching out southward and westward along the river banks. The march of peace brought
with it increased population and prosperity. The admin-
istrations of Governors Tynte and Hyde had witnessed
one of the bloodiest wars ever carried on in the territory
now known as North Carolina, but Governor Eden, who,
in 1714, was appointed Hyde's successor by the Lords
Proprietors, was to usher in a new era of peace and well-
being in the colony. The General Assembly, over which
Governor Eden presided in 1715, was destined to insti-
gate many legislative measures for the economic and
political progress of the colony.

It was during the meeting of this legislative body, in
1715, that the first direct tax was levied on the inhabitants of North Carolina, at least so far as any record in
existence today shows;[3] this took the dual form of a poll
and a land tax.[4] The latter tax will be discussed in a
later Chapter; in this Chapter attention will be confined to
a survey of the poll tax in North Carolina during the
colonial period.

Description and Basis of the Poll Tax. The poll tax
derived its name from the object of its imposition. The
word "poll" is derived from the Middle English noun,
pol, or *polle,* which is related to the Low German word,
polle, meaning, *the head.*[5] Bouvier defines poll as "A
head; hence poll-tax is the name of a tax imposed upon
the people at so much a head."[6] The poll tax, therefore,

---

[3] Hyde's appointment as Governor in 1712 marked the entire separation of the government of North Carolina from that of South Carolina.
Colonial Records, Vol. I, Prefatory Notes, p. xxxi.

[4] Clarke's *Laws of North Carolina,* Vol. 23, pp. 90–92.

[5] Webster's *International Dictionary.*

[6] Bouvier's *Law Dictionary,* p. 952.

is a "capitation tax; a tax assessed on every head, i.e., on every male of a certain age, etc., according to statute." [7] When social conditions in the colony were crude and characterized by a rigid simplicity, a tax on the individual rather than on his property, was considered fair, for "the social obligations of the members of the clan or the state" at that time, were "conceived to be equal." [8] When slaves were introduced into the colony the poll tax applied to them also; this virtually made the poll a tax on a certain type of property; this phase will be discussed later. Professor Seligman's characterization of the poll tax in primitive society may be applied to the colony in the Province of North Carolina. "In primitive society," he says, "There is a certain rough equality in the personal status and the personal abilities of the individual. Hence, the idea of the poll or capitation tax, which is the first rude manifestation of the equities of taxation." [9] Therefore the poll tax was naturally considered a fitting type of assessment to be used for obtaining revenue in colonial North Carolina.

What rôle did the poll tax play in the taxation system of North Carolina during the colonial period? The quantitative answer to this question would show that during this era the poll tax occupied a more important place in the revenue system of North Carolina than it did in any of the neighboring states. The expenses connected with governing the colony of North Carolina in the eighteenth century, unlike those in practically all the other southern states where they were met principally by money derived from indirect taxation, were defrayed mainly by the proceeds from the poll tax. In this respect North Carolina resembled the New England states, notwithstanding the

---

[7] Bouvier's *Law Dictionary*, p. 952.
[8] Seligman, E. R. A., *Essays in Taxation*, p. 10.
[9] *Ibid.*, p. 10.

fact that her method of imposing the tax was entirely different.[10]   That North Carolina relied more and more upon her poll tax for income as the decades passed in the colonial period may partially be explained by her geographical position and peculiarities.   Her coast was practically inaccessible for large ships; her geological formation made commerce by this route dangerous; her mountains and streams, running northward and southward, invited traders from Virginia and South Carolina.   Migration to North Carolina was over the land route, although traveling by land was a difficult task in those days when forests were dense and traveling facilities primitive and crude.   In consequence, her imports and exports being less extensive than those in Virginia, South Carolina, and other southern states, North Carolina was compelled to seek other sources to supplement her taxation system.   She found the poll tax a successful expedient for a great many years.

This levy was imposed equally upon all taxable persons; it fell in the same amount upon the rich and the poor.   The inhabitants of North Carolina during the colonial period have been divided into four distinct groups; the gentry, the yeomanry, white servants, and slaves.   Of the first class, the chief forms of wealth were land and slaves.   To this class belonged the wealthy plantation owners, whose numbers in North Carolina were never so large as in Virginia; in fact the gentry formed a very small part of North Carolina's population.   To the yeomanry, the largest class in the social division of

---

[10] In New England local self-government was the policy pursued, with the county as the unit.   Taxes were levied by each county according to its needs.   In North Carolina the central government, through the General Assembly, levied the taxes throughout the colony.

colonial North Carolina, belonged landowners on a smaller scale. Unlike the planter, who only supervised his plantation, the yeoman worked his land himself. Brickell tells us somewhere that "yeomen often equalized with the negro in hard labor." [11] Then there was the indentured servant class, or white servants, who, after completing their term of service, became free, some of them afterwards becoming yeomen; this class, like the gentry, formed a comparatively small group in North Carolina. The slave class was composed of Indians and negroes, the latter, however, being in the great majority. The planter class owned practically all the slaves, for its aristocracy was built on slave labor; and in the eastern part of the state, where the planters lived, land was more suitable for the production of crops worked by slave labor. Next in numbers to the yeomanry, was the slave class; the former was the largest class, it paid the largest part of the poll tax, for this tax was imposed upon individuals.

The debts incurred during the Tuscarora War were paid by a poll tax,[12] through which all of the great wars, from this date until the Revolution against England, were financed. From 1715 onward the poll tax continued to bear the heaviest of the governmental expenditures, especially for outstanding emergencies.

The principle underlying the levy of the poll tax during the colonial era must be clearly conceived and borne in mind. During the entire colonial period this tax was levied uniformly upon every person subject to it; a wealthy landowner with hundreds of slaves paid the same

[11] Brickell, John, *Natural History of North Carolina.*
[12] A small land tax supplemented the poll tax at this time. Clarke's *Laws of North Carolina*, Vol. 23, p. 90.

amount for each of his slaves as he did for himself. Personal liability was the basis for this form of taxation and the value of the slave was not considered; tax was imposed merely on numbers.

The feudal influence is traceable even in the term designating the tax; it was called a tithe, was a capitation tax on a person, and was not regulated by the amount of his possessions. Taxable persons were designated as "tythables." At the sitting of the Assembly in 1715, an act was passed to "ascertain what persons were tythables," and "to direct the method to be observed in taking the list of them." [13] The idea of exemption for minimum of subsistence was recognized, though not stated legally. Persons who were paupers, or individuals, who, for some reason, were financially incapacitated, were exempted by laws made to apply specifically to the case or cases under discussion at a specific time. A list, to be used as a basis for collection, was taken of the remaining eligible people in the province, and only one exception to this general condition appeared among the laws: this occurred in 1715 when the Assembly and Lords Proprietors passed an act "Exempting New-Comers from Paying Levys for One Year." [14]

One fact must not be overlooked. The taxes were generally paid in commodities during the earlier part of this period, because money was scarce in the colony; during the latter part of the colonial era, however, proclamation money, which was being issued as legal tender, was used. A law was passed in 1715 rating a list of staple commodities in sterling, as follows: [15]

---

[13] Clarke's *Laws of North Carolina,* Vol. 23, pp. 72–75.
[14] *Ibid.,* Vol. 25, p. 120.
[15] *Ibid.,* Vol. 23, p. 54.

	£	s	d
Tobacco per cwt.	o	10	o
Indyan Corn per Bush.		1	8
Wheat		3	6
Tallow Fryed, per lb.			5
Leather Tanned and Uncured, per lb.....			8
Beaver and other Skins per lb.		2	6
Wild Cat Skins per piece		1	o
Butter per lb.			6
Cheese per lb.			4
Buck & Doe Skins (raw) per lb.			9
Buck & Doe Skins (dressed) per lb.		2	6
Feathers per lb.		1	4
Pitch (full gauged) per Barl	1	o	o
Whale Oil	1	10	o
Porke	2	5	o
Beef	1	10	o

In 1731, these commodities were rerated, eliminating butter and cheese, and adding tar, rice, and turpentine.[16] This new list of commodities was used not only for paying quit-rents and fees, but also for paying taxes until the year 1748, when proclamation money was declared to be the only medium of exchange to be accepted for taxes.

Public Expenditures and Uses of the Poll Tax. The chief uses for which the poll tax was levied in the colonial period in North Carolina, may be arranged in four classifications. In the first place, certain governmental expenditures were met with some of the income from the poll tax. In the second place, wars necessitated lavish expenditures for the equipment and sustenance of troops and the payment of officers, and the poll tax was a convenient means of raising the sums needed. In the third place, debts were incurred which required the raising of extra funds in some manner for their payment; the poll tax became a popular source for the relief of this exigency also. In

[16] *Colonial Records,* Vol. III, p. 168.

the fourth place, most local expenditures in the separate counties were paid by a special poll tax, levied on the inhabitants in the particular locality for which it was to be used.

In such a primitive community as the one in Albemarle public expenditures were simple and meager. Generally speaking, each class of public officials had a specific source from which to obtain support. The Governor's salary, which was probably the largest fixed expenditure for any one phase of the government of the colony, was paid from the quit-rents, as we have seen; while the Treasurer and many other officials imposed fees and also received part of the impost duties on liquors for their upkeep. This condition prevailed throughout the colonial period in North Carolina. The expenses of the judiciary department were sometimes met through the poll tax. An instance of this occurred in the November session of the General Assembly in 1758, when a special act was passed levying a poll tax of one shilling and eightpence for a period of four years for the payment of the salaries of the Chief Justice and Attorney General and other "contingent charges of the government." [17] In 1761 an additional poll tax of two shillings, for the same purpose, was levied for a period of five years.[18]

In addition to occasional provisions for the salaries of governmental officials, measures had to be taken by the government for the protection and defense of the settlers against enemies. As wars with the Indians were not infrequent occurrences in the region which developed into the territory of North Carolina, money, or the equivalent of money, was needed for building forts, for raising and equipping an army of some sort, and for carrying on

[17] Clarke's *Laws of North Carolina,* Vol. 23, p. 494.
[18] *Ibid.,* Vol. 23, p. 542

campaigns against the hostile forces. During the eighteenth century colonial Carolina levied poll taxes for this purpose. As an illustration, a tax of two shillings per poll was levied in 1755 for five years for defraying expenses in waging war against the French and Indians. The following year a poll tax of two shillings was placed on the inhabitants "for granting to his Majesty an Aid of £3,400 to defray the Expenses of erecting a Fort, raising and paying Two Companies, for the Defense of the Western Frontier" [19] of the province. Another tax of four shillings, sixpence per poll, was granted in 1757 for paying the forces.[20] As will be seen later, instances of this kind occurred frequently throughout the period under discussion.

As governmental expenditures of various types increased with the growth of the colony, a sinking fund was often essential for settling the debts which necessarily accrued. The poll tax was used in almost every case of this kind. Partially as a result of the Tuscarora War, the government in 1714 owed £24,000, and the following year a tax of fifteen shillings per toll was levied "for raising the sum of two thousand pounds annually till the public debts are answered and paid and for the better encouraging the Currency of the Public bills of Credit." [21] This year marked the beginning of the imposition of the poll tax, which was afterward used extensively for the liquidation of public debts.

By 1740 the counties had multiplied and developed to such an extent that funds for specific local expenditures were often needed; this brought into existence a fourth charge upon the inhabitants of the colony. Public

[19] Clarke's *Laws of North Carolina,* Vol. 25, pp. 331–333.
[20] *Ibid.,* Vol. 25, p. 350.
[21] *Ibid.,* Vol. 23, p. 91.

granaries and warehouses for storing tobacco, corn, and other mediums of payment had been erected, and the expenses incurred were usually met by a poll tax levied upon the citizens of the county. In this year, for instance, the Assembly placed a poll tax "not exceeding 1 shilling" for one year upon the taxable people of Bath "for building a warehouse." [22] These local expenditures formed such an important phase of the colony's system of finances that the subject will be dealt with later in a separate chapter. It is sufficient to note here that practically all of these local expenditures were defrayed by revenue collected from the poll tax.

In a description of conditions in North Carolina sent to the Lords Commissioners for Trade and Plantations in England, about 1762, was an account of the taxes. In this report the uses of the poll tax were summarized in the following sentence: "The Several Taxes during their Continuance are appropriated to sink the paper Currency and to repay those which were issued and if His Majesty approved of their being reissued were appropriated to purchase Glebes, build publick schools, or to pay the Assistant Justices and Attorneys General." [23] At this point the fact should be mentioned that the colonies insisted upon exercising exclusive power in the realm of direct taxation. The Lower House, which was composed of the representatives of the people as complementary to the representatives of the Lords Proprietors, or royal interests, in the Upper House, claimed the prerogative of originating all bills for taxation. Any amendment to be made to these bills, had also to be introduced from the Lower House, in accordance with the custom brought over from England. The colonists argued that they should

[22] Clarke's *Laws of North Carolina*, Vol. 23, p. 152.
[23] *Colonial Records*, Vol. VI, p. 619.

be the source from which the bills should spring, since they were the people who were to pay these taxes, and were the ones for whose benefit they were supposed to be levied. To this rule they clung tenaciously and triumphantly.

Historical Development. As has been stated before the first recorded imposition of a poll tax upon the inhabitants of the province of North Carolina was in 1715. At that time the tax, which was fifteen shillings per tythable, was levied in order to pay a debt for which the state had become liable as a result of the Tuscarora War, and to meet other expenditures. The Yemassee Indians were making war on the colonists in South Carolina. Two years before, in 1711, when the Tuscarora Indians were ravaging the North Carolina settlers, their southern neighbors had promptly sent help; this courtesy North Carolina now returned by sending aid to South Carolina; this necessitated an additional expense for the government. The government of North Carolina, in 1714, had issued £24,000 in Bills of Credit,[24] which, with the aid of the poll and other taxes, had in 1717, been reduced to £16,000.[25] The rate of fifteen shillings per poll remained in force for five years. Ashe gave evidence of the continued prosperity of the colony in his statement in 1718 that "there were about one million acres held subject to quit-rents, and there were about two thousand tithables in the colony; and despite the orders, the people were spreading out in Craven and up the Neuse and along the Roanoke."[26] The affairs of the province, on the whole, had continued quiet and the administration had been successful in attaining a smoothly running governmental

[24] *Colonial Records,* Vol. II, Prefatory Notes, p. v.
[25] *Ibid.,* p. v.
[26] Ashe, S. A., *History of North Carolina,* Vol. I, p. 206.

machine, the finances of which were in a favorable condition. When the General Assembly met in August, 1720, it therefore reduced the poll tax "from 15 shillings per tythable to 10 shillings per tythable." [27]

In March, 1722, Governor Eden died, at the height of a prosperous administration. [28] Edenton had become the capital, and the territory west of the Chowan had become so populous that it had been established as the Precinct of Bertie. [29] Southward, along the coast, the town of Beaufort was incorporated as a seaport and Carteret Precinct was established. [30] The growth and commercial activities of the province were further advanced by an act passed to encourage a settlement at Ocracoke Inlet, where navigation was favorable. Public bills of credit, which were still used for raising money with the poll tax as the chief means of retiring them, had in 1722 been reduced to £12,000 and the poll tax was lowered to five shillings per taxable yearly.

From 1723 to 1734 there seem to have been no taxation bills passed by the Assembly. This was a period during which many practical disputes kept the Assembly divided,—Burrington, with his lack of tact, and Everard, with his weak administration, were governors during this period. With the entrance of Burrington as Governor of the province, political strife began to brew, and he soon made the Assembly antagonistic to all of his plans. He was deposed by Sir Richard Everard, whom he in turn displaced. This conflict in governmental affairs in Albemarle continued for many years and probably gave impetus to the settlement of the Cape Fear region, which,

[27] Clarke's *Laws of North Carolina*, Vol. 25, p. 162.
[28] Ashe, S. A., *History of North Carolina*, Vol. I, p. 206.
[29] *Ibid.*, p. 207.
[30] *Colonial Records*, Vol. II, pp. 458–459.

together with the lands limited by South Carolina, was included when Carteret Precinct was formed. Adjoining the territory of Bath County, which stretched from the Albemarle Sound southward as far as any settlement was made in Carteret Precinct Maurice Moore on June 3, 1725, received the first grant of 1,500 acres of land on the west bank of the river, sixteen miles below the spot now known as Wilmington and adjoining the territory of Bath County, which stretched from the Albemarle Sound southward as far as any settlement was made in Carteret Precinct. There he established the town of Brunswick where, in response to his urging, people began to settle on both sides of the river, thus opening another port and harbor to the province.

With the King's purchase of Carolina in 1729, a currency bill had been passed by the government:[31] £10,000 to be applied to the redemption of the former bills of credit issued by the government, and the remaining £20,000 to be loaned to the various precincts, according to their needs. These loans were to be repaid in fifteen years in equal payments and were made at six per cent interest, with land as security. Paper money then came into existence, and was in use at the time when the Crown purchased Carolina.

With the passing of the Lords Proprietors and their lax and indifferent control, the province of North Carolina was destined to come under a different kind of supervision. While there was no apparent change in the government, yet the relationship between England and this province was somewhat altered; by virtue of the dignity of its position the prestige of the royal authority in this territory was greater than that of the Lords Proprietors. The Crown took a closer interest in the affairs of the

[31] *Colonial Records,* Vol. II, Prefatory Notes, p. v.

colony, for England was planning to solidify all of her
colonies into a better organized and more compact
empire, with herself as the center of the organization.
In order to accomplish this object, she was compelled to
examine into the economic and political conditions of
these colonies, of which one was North Carolina, and in
many cases to develop and build them up. In comparison
with Virginia and South Carolina, North Carolina's
growth had at this time been slow, chiefly because access
to the early plantations near the Albemarle Sound was
intricate and hazardous, while the entire coast of North
Carolina was dangerous and was devoid of any good
harbors. Naturally, therefore, settlers coming from
Europe sought the coasts of other states on which to
land. Life, however, was easy and agreeable, even
though the scattered population made social advantages
difficult of attainment. Not even religious centers, with
their customarily socializing influence, existed in this
society—only the Quakers being organized—for the
people as a whole were not religious. Industries were
not numerous, but, in addition to agricultural pursuits,
shipbuilding was carried on to a certain extent in the
province.[32] There were in 1729 about 30,000 people
in the colony, a small population in comparison with that
of other states. Of these inhabitants many were poor,
and conveniences attendant upon a more developed social
stage were conspicuously lacking for a majority of the
people. Since land was cheap and labor expensive, they
lived in rude cabins, and cleared the land for cultivation
by manual labor. The transfer of the colony from the
Lords Proprietors to the Crown, however, resulted immediately in greater development. As the Cape Fear
River, with its port, opened that section of the country

[32] *Colonial Records,* Vol. II, p. 241.

to settlement, immigration there was large. In a few years this area surpassed the older settlement around Albemarle in commercial and industrial importance; the colony was growing more rapidly than ever before in its history.

During Burrington's second administration (from 1731 to 1734) owing to factional disputes in the government, no act was passed which was recognized as law. With the arrival of Governor Johnston, however, more progress was made, and in 1734, an act for granting £14,150, 3s. 2d., "for the service of the Public of this Province," was passed with a provision for "laying a tax on the inhabitants," for its payment.[33] While the amount of this tax is not recorded, there is an indication that the poll tax was bearing heavily on the poorer classes in the province at this time, for the Assembly passed an act laying a duty on Liquors for defraying the contingent charges of government and "to make the poll tax on the poorer inhabitants more easy." [34] This would suggest that the poll tax had been in operation throughout this period, although attempts to evade it had been made by concealing some of the tithables in the counties. There were laws passed from time to time in an effort to counteract the effects of this condition; the first law of this type was recorded in 1738, and was enacted in conjunction with the passage of an act" for granting to his Majesty a poll-tax of five shillings per head," to be laid on the taxable inhabitants of the province.[35]

From 1715 to 1740, affairs in the province were comparatively peaceful; no great wars came to disturb the

[33] Clarke's *Laws of North Carolina,* Vol. 23, p. 121.
[34] *Ibid.,* Vol. 23, p. 117.
[35] *Ibid.,* Vol. 23, p. 122.

inhabitants, and the poll taxes levied during this period were for the payment of back debts incurred in former wars, and for defraying current governmental expenses. In 1740, however, came the Spanish War, or as it is popularly known, "The War of Jenkin's Ear," followed, during the succeeding decade and a half, by wars of all sorts which came to disturb the people of North Carolina. The Assembly appropriated £12,000 in sterling to the King for the maintenance and transportation of troops to the fields of battle,[36] and in one year a poll tax of three shillings, proclamation money, was levied on the inhabitants for this purpose.[37] Following this war, there were several Spanish invasions of the coast of North Carolina, the most notable of which occurred in the years of 1741, 1744, 1747 and 1748. In the year last mentioned, the Spanish intruders were successfully driven away by the colonists, and, in order to fortify itself against the enemy, the colony issued new bills of credit and built new houses as receptacles for military stores. In 1743 a poll tax of eightpence, proclamation money, was levied on the people "for providing proper magazines of ammunition in the several counties of this province," [38] and in 1745 a tax of one shilling, proclamation money, was levied for eight years for the purpose of making some "new current Bills of Credit." [39] In April, 1748 a bill for the issue of £6,000 in bills of credit was passed in the Assembly in order to build two large forts, one at Cape Fear and one at Ocracoke, to aid in repelling the Spanish enemy,[40] together with a levy of one shilling, proclamation

---

[36] *Colonial Records*, Vol. IV, p. 421.
[37] Clarke's *Laws of North Carolina*, Vol. 23, p. 151.
[38] *Ibid.*, Vol. 25, pp. 232–233.
[39] *Ibid.*, Vol. 25, pp. 234–235.
[40] *Ibid.*, Vol. 23, pp. 292–294.

money, for retiring these and other bills issued at that time. It is interesting to note that this was likewise the year in which the law was enacted making all taxes payable in proclamation money, and refusing to accept commodities for this purpose. This indicates that money had become plentiful in the province. By the end of that year, North Carolina had rid itself of Spanish invaders and was free, for a brief time, to direct attention to internal matters.

During the decade prior to the middle of the eighteenth century, settlers had begun to come in great numbers to North Carolina. The Scotch-Irish came first, some from Charleston where they had landed in America, but the majority of them from Pennsylvania, where they had landed at Philadelphia. By 1745 the territory between the Catawba and Yadkin rivers in North Carolina had become populated with Scotch-Irish immigrants; these were soon followed by an influx of Pennsylvania Dutch, of German extraction, who had come to settle in North Carolina around the region now known as Winston-Salem.[41] A traveler [42] in the western part of the colony said in 1746 that there were not more than one hundred fighting men in this section between Virginia and South Carolina; seven years later, however, he estimated this number as thirty times greater, and said that it was increasing daily.[43] The growth of these and other interior settlements was so rapid that the government was for a few years scarcely aware of it. Then new counties began to be formed; that of Orange, for instance, in 1752, the year in which Bishop Spangenberg, making a journey through the western part of North Carolina,

[41] *Colonial Records,* Vol. IV, Prefatory Notes, p. xxi.
[42] Matthew Rowan.
[43] *Colonial Records,* Vol. V, p. 24.

found many Indians and hunters located there.[44] Although population in this section was at that time increasing by leaps and bounds, the voice of the government still came from the east, around Edenton, Newbern and the Cape Fear region, where the old planters, possessing the wealth of the colony, held the balance of power in political life.

Despite all dissensions over the seat of government in the case of Edenton versus Newbern, the latter town was to receive that honor. In 1749 an act was passed fixing the seat of government at Newbern and for "keeping public offices."[45] To defray expenses attendant on this act, a tax of fourpence, proclamation money, per poll was placed on each taxable for three years. To the act above, another clause was added in 1750 for appointing Circuit Courts and defraying their expenses,[46] together with the levy for this purpose of a poll tax of twopence for two years. In 1753 the act of 1749, with the poll tax of fourpence per year for fixing the seat of government and defraying officers' expenses, was continued for three years longer.[47]

North Carolina was again involved in war in 1754 when the French invaded the western part of Virginia, and that state called upon North Carolina for help.[48] In February the General Assembly granted to the King an aid of £40,000 in public bills of credit for organizing troops, building forts, and meeting other expenses in the province, but principally for sending forces to assist the colony of Virginia.[49] At that time a tax of one shilling per

---

[44] *Colonial Records*, Vol. IV, p. 1312.
[45] Clarke's *Laws of North Carolina*, Vol. 23, p. 329
[46] *Ibid.*, Vol. 23, pp. 347–348.
[47] *Ibid.*, Vol. 25, pp. 254–255.
[48] *Colonial Records*, Vol. V, p. 392.
[49] Clarke's *Laws of North Carolina*, Vol. 23, pp. 392–398.

poll was levied in North Carolina for sinking this fund. As has been mentioned previously, there was another tax of one shilling, sixpence, in proclamation money, levied on the poll annually for four years for raising funds to pay the salaries of the Chief Justice and Attorney General, and for other governmental purposes.[50]

A poll of two shillings per taxable was levied in 1755 on the North Carolina inhabitants for a period of five years for carrying on war against the French and Indians.[51] In 1756 an additional act for granting to "His Majesty" £3,400 for erecting a fort and for paying and raising two companies for the defense of the western frontier, caused a levy, in addition to a liquor tax, of a poll tax of two shillings for the following year.[52] During the next year the French and Indian War spread to South Carolina; North Carolina sent aid to that province also. A tax of four shillings, sixpence was placed on each poll in North Carolina in May, 1757, for defraying war expenses and for paying the principal and interest on the notes and public bills of credit issued by the government.[53] This remained in force until 1760 throughout the province, and, in addition, another poll tax of two shillings was imposed in 1757 for retiring some notes in the province.[54] In 1758 and 1759 the poll tax of four shillings, sixpence, with a liquor tax, was used for paying troops to be joined under Brigadier-General Forbes and for placing a garrison in the forts on the sea coast.[55] In 1758 a poll tax of one shilling, eightpence, was levied to continue in effect for four years for paying

[50] Clarke's *Laws of North Carolina*, Vol. 25, pp. 309–310.
[51] *Ibid.*, Vol. 23, pp. 422–424.
[52] *Ibid.*, Vol. 25, pp. 331–333.
[53] *Ibid.*, Vol. 25, pp. 345–348.
[54] *Ibid.*, Vol. 25, pp. 351–352.
[55] *Ibid.*, Vol. 25, pp. 361–364.

the Chief Justice's and Attorney General's salaries, "and other contingent charges of government." [56]

An act passed in 1759, levied a poll tax of one shilling, eightpence on the taxables of North Carolina, to be collected annually in 1761, 1762, and 1763, for replacing £5,500 which had been used in paying the militia in the province; [57] and again in 1760, after the French and Indian War had been over for about two years, a poll tax of one shilling was levied in North Carolina to continue until the outstanding bills of credit should be paid. [58]   This tax was in 1761 raised to two shillings, which was to continue for five years. [59]   The territory between the Catawba and the Yadkin rivers in the western part of the country having been laid waste by the Cherokee Indians in 1760, troops to be equipped for war were immediately voted for the service of the King. [60]   Later, in November, it was the intention of the Assembly to send men to aid Virginia and South Carolina against this common enemy, but the Governor, for a minor reason, refused to let the bill pass. [61]   It was not long, however, before the war ceased in North Carolina, and no more troops were necessary.   This war and an increase in the salaries of the Chief Justice and Attorney General caused the increase in the poll tax in that year.

A bill which had been passed in the Assembly in the year 1761, granting the King £20,000 in proclamation money for the upkeep of the army, [62] was to take effect in January of 1764, when a poll tax of two shillings was to

[56] Clarke's *Laws of North Carolina*, Vol. 23, p. 494.
[57] *Ibid.*, Vol. 25, p. 395.
[58] *Ibid.*, Vol. 23, p. 518.
[59] *Ibid.*, Vol. 23, p. 542.
[60] *Colonial Records*, Vol. VI, p. 439.
[61] *Ibid.*, Vol. VI, p. 513.
[62] Clarke's *Laws of North Carolina*, Vol. 25, pp. 457–458.

be collected from the people of North Carolina until the entire sum should be paid. It was also voted in 1764 to continue for two years longer the poll tax of one shilling, sixpence, for paying the Chief Justice's and Attorney General's salaries.[63] The Peace of Paris, signed in 1762, freed the English subjects in America from fear of foreign foes, so that they could devote themselves more exclusively to fostering affairs at home. Although the Cherokee War had checked the tide of immigration to western North Carolina, which had begun about ten years before, at this time, nevertheless, the population of North Carolina was about 110,000 people, 100,000 white and 10,-000 negroes.[64] Forty saw-mills along the Cape Fear River were estimated to produce annually about 30,000,-000 feet of lumber, and about 36,000 barrels of naval stores were exported annually from this region.[65] The Indians, who by this time, had been reduced in number and corralled in a few reservations in North Carolina, were henceforth to play an inconspicuous part in the colony.[66] The educational facilities of the colony were limited to the wealthy, and although attempts were made to start free schools, these efforts all met with failure.[67]

Although the colonies had, until 1763, readily made liberal grants of money to the King for carrying on wars and other expenses of the Crown—in the form of spontaneous offerings, not exactings—the idea was held in England, that the colonies should contribute funds, imposed by law in a systematic manner, to be used for the partial maintenance of the British Empire. The troops

[63] Clarke's *Laws of North Carolina,* Vol. 23, p. 617.
[64] *Colonial Records,* Vol. VI, pp. 1027–2040.
[65] *Ibid.,* Vol. VI, p. 1030.
[66] *Ibid.,* Vol. VI., pp. 616, 995, 1041.
[67] *Ibid.,* Vol. VI, p. 1006.

in America were to be supported by these colonies and, since most of the lands of the colonies had been purchased by the Crown, their governments were to be reorganized and the salaries of officials placed on a more certain basis. With these and other objects in view, the subject was being agitated by discussion in England, when, in October, 1763, Henry McCulloh, who had been connected with colonial affairs for years, proposed a Stamp Act as a means of raising the necessary money.[68] This act was destined to be far-reaching in its effects.

The people in the American colonies were greatly agitated; they argued that the restrictions concerning imports and exports, which England had heretofore imposed on her colonies had had as their object the increase and regulation of commerce, while the newly proposed act was inspired by an entirely different consideration. Parliament proposed to tax the colonies for the purpose of obtaining revenue, and gradually, as the American colonists examined the question, they became hostile to the proposal. At the last meeting of the North Carolina General Assembly in October, 1764, that body definitely announced its views on the subject. To the opening address of the Governor, who represented the Crown, the House's reply was caustic; it declared that it did not welcome the idea of having its commerce burdened with new taxes and impositions without its privity and consent, and against what its members esteemed their inherent right and exclusive privilege of imposing their own taxes. For about ten years such discussions as these were to continue, finally to terminate in war. The spirit of the Assembly during this session is reflected in an episode concerning the printing of the laws. The Gov-

---

[68] *Colonial Records,* Vol, VI, p. 1021.

ernor and Council appointed a printer for this duty, call-
ing him "His Majesty's Printer." When the House
heard of this, it asserted that there was no such office,
and appointed another person to print the laws. When
the Governor claimed the right to order payment out
of the funds of the colony, the House said that no money
should be paid out of the Treasury "by order of the
Governor and Council without the concurrence or direc-
tion of this house."[69] The representatives of the people
thus kept control of the finances of the colony.

In 1766 a vote was passed authorizing the erection of a
beautiful new building in Newbern for the residence of
the Governor. In addition to the liquor tax imposed for
this purpose, there was a poll tax of eightpence in proclamation money levied for two years upon the people
of the province to meet the expense of building this edi-
fice.[70] In 1767, in addition to this tax on the poll for
building the Governor's mansion, there was levied another tax of two shillings per poll for three years.[71] The
following year, in 1768, the peace was disturbed by the
War of the Regulators in the western part of the state.
The poll tax was used for paying the expenses of the
colony in subduing these insurgents, and at the November session of the Assembly a tax of two shillings on the
poll, in proclamation money, was laid on the colonists to
begin in 1771 and to continue until the debt of £20,000,
incurred during the insurrection, should be paid.[72]

The last record of any poll tax enacted for the use
of the central government in North Carolina during the
colonial period is that of the year 1771. This was an

69 *Colonial Records,* Vol. VI, pp. 1311–1318.
70 Clarke's *Laws of North Carolina,* Vol. 23, pp. 664–665
71 *Ibid.,* Vol. 23, pp. 711–713.
72 *Ibid.,* Vol. 23, pp. 781–783.

"Act for imposing a tax of Two Shillings, Proclamation Money, per Poll on all Taxable Persons within this Province, and for granting the money arising from such Tax to his Majesty, his Heirs and Successors, to be applied as hereinafter directed." [73] This was to have continued for a period of ten years, and was to be used for redeeming debenture bills to the amount of £60,000' but, with the beginning of hostilities against England, this act became void.

The Declaration of the Mecklenburg Independence, however, did not put an end to the levy of poll taxes in North Carolina. They merely ceased to be levied for his Majesty's benefit, and the government of North Carolina continued to use this form of tax for raising funds for the state.

Importance and General Effect. As the colonial era advanced, the poll tax in North Carolina bore an increasing percentage of the expenses connected with the government. The rates per poll, collectively speaking, ranged anywhere from three shillings in 1740 to sixteen shillings and fourpence per taxable in 1760.[74] This tax was comparatively easy to collect, although not immune from evasion, as some of the laws of that period show, for it was relatively more difficult to conceal persons than things. Import and export duties on articles may be easily evaded by smuggling, as we have seen, but a tax on persons who live in the country cannot be so readily avoided. The Sheriffs in the counties made proper lists of taxables and sent them to the Secretary of the Colony, who supervised the collection of the tax on the basis of these lists. As an illustration of the lists of taxables

[73] Clarke's *Laws of North Carolina*, Vol. 23, pp. 850–851.
[74] *Colonial Records*, Vol. VI, p. 619.

made in North Carolina during this period, the following table is representative: [75]

A GENERAL LIST OF TAXABLES AS RET[D] INTO THE SECRETARY'S OFFICE FOR THE YEAR OF 1754.

Counties	Clerks	White Men	Black Males	Black Fems.	Total
Anson K.	Henry Nendry	810	40	20	870 [1]
Beaufort K. G.	Walley Chaina	637	267	218 }	1,306
184 not distinguished		120	40	24 }	
Bertia G.	Saml. Armes	1,220	289	200	1,709 [2]
Bladen K.	Thos. Robison	338	226	120	684
Carteret K.	Geo. Reed				400 [1]
Chowan G.	Wm. Halsey				1481 [3]
Craven K.	Sol. Rew	870	468	308	1,646
Cumberland K.	Tos. Jones				850 [1]
Currituck K.	G. Shergold	470	80	70	629 [1]
Duplin K.	Dickson	560	105	63	628
Edgecomb G.	Benj. Wynns	1,611	508	416	2,535
Granville G.	Danl. Weldon	779	261	165	1,205
Hyde K. G.	Saml. Sinclare	237	100	83	420
Johnston K. G.	Chas. Young				1,425
New Han'r	Isaac Faries	362	799	575	1,736
Northampton, G.	John Edwards	902	510	324	1,736
Onslow K.	Will M. Crag	448	151	96	695
Orange G.	R'D Caswell	950	35	15	1,000 [4]
Pasquotank G.	Thos. Taylor	563	266	100	929
Perquimans G.	R'd Clayton				1,117
Rowan G.	John Dunn	1116	30	24	1,170
Tyrrell G.	Evan Jones	500	100	90	690 [3]
		12,393	4,275	2,911	24,861
				4,275	
				7,186	

1 Computed.
2 Not Dist. in return.
3 Not distingh'd.
4 Not ret'd.

The white tithables were only the males from 18 years upward; women and those under the age of 18, both

75 *Colonial Records,* Vol. V, p. 320.

males and females were not tithes; and the negroes or blacks were tithables from 16 years upward, both males and females.[76]

As the colony grew and the population spread westward, the wealthy planters in the east who had hitherto had the sole voice in political affairs, began to realize that their less wealthy but energetic fellow colonists in the west were becoming influential in such matters. There was as yet no tax on real estate, and the poll tax, the amount of which was placed on all persons alike, was a greater burden on the poor inhabitants of the west than on the planters of the east. It is true that the poll tax virtually became a property tax on the planters as this class was compelled to pay on each slave; but a tax on land, which was more plentiful than slaves, or a tax on any other property, would have fallen more heavily upon this class. The poll tax was scattered and actually took a higher rate of money, in proportion to income, from the non-property owners than from the property owners. The planter class, which was at first responsible for the laws, benefited considerably by paying a poll tax alone. Import duties on wines and liquors, however, fell almost exclusively upon this class, for it was the only one able to buy these products; whenever more emphasis could be placed on the poll and less on import duties, therefore, this class was loud in its assent.

About the end of the decade after the middle of the eighteenth century, there was such a protest raised in the west against the poll tax that, in 1769, an investigation of the financial affairs of the colony was made. This was the period in which the regulators created trouble. People thought they were paying more taxes than ever reached the public treasury, and the belief that the tax officials

[76] *Colonial Records,* Vol. V, p. 565.

were corrupt and dishonest seemed to prevail through the state. This view was shared by Governor Tryon. As a result of this wide-spread opinion, the Assembly appointed a representative to investigate the matter and three reports were made: one showed that the sheriffs were delinquent in turning over the amounts which they were supposed to have collected; a second report indicated that the taxes levied exceeded the amount of currency issued to be retired by these taxes; a third report gave a table showing the "taxables and taxes paid" by counties from 1748 to 1770.[77] Although these were poll taxes, not all records of the laws imposing these taxes are in existence. The tax of £1 for the sinking fund, as shown in the table, had its origin in 1748; it was doubled in 1763 and again in the following year—a fact which is not shown in the statutes—while in 1768 it seems to have been diminished to its original rate of £1, another fact which is not verified by the law records. The school tax from 1755 to 1761 inclusive, as shown in the table, yielded an income of about £900 per year as Governor Dobbs stated, but it was never used for the purpose intended, because the expenses of conducting the French and Indian War absorbed it and the public school was not established at that time. The table gives a list of counties from which no taxes were collected during part of this time, but many of these counties either were not in existence during the time the table shows no taxes, or else kept no tax records. The unarmed rebellion of 1748 probably explains the absence of any tax report at that time for Chowan, Pasquotank, Perquimans and Tyrrell counties. Although the table does not give a complete

[77] Boyd, W. K., A Table of North Carolina Taxes, 1748–1770. *The North Carolina Historical Review*, Vol. III, No. 3, July, 1926, pp. 475–476.

account of the taxes imposed during this period, it nevertheless reveals a number of valuable points.

The colony arrived at the threshold of the Revolution which was to bring independence. Although North
Carolina, through the poll tax, had financed many wars
and uprisings on her soil, the Revolution against England
would involve a struggle more deadly and more costly than
any she had ever known. The poll tax, moreover, was
becoming increasingly unpopular with the masses. Nevertheless, North Carolina not only needed the aid of a
poll tax, but she needed some other tax also. With the
introduction of the property tax, therefore, the poll tax
came up for further debate but with a different emphasis.
The Revolution thus marked the beginning of a new
epoch in taxation in North Carolina.

CHAPTER V

LAND AND MISCELLANEOUS TAXES

THE taxation system in North Carolina during the colonial period was composed principally of the poll tax and duties on imports and exports. There were, however, other minor types of taxes levied which, although unimportant in their effect at that time, may be said to have contained the germs of the taxation systems which developed later in the state. At all events, this entire colonial system disclosed no regularity or uniformity as to the time, the amount, or the kind of levy. The Assembly had only one criterion by which to work—that was to raise the money needed at the particular time, from whatever source it could be obtained. Levying taxes whenever the exigencies of the occasion demanded, stating the amount necessary to defray the charge of the specific object in view, and demanding this in the form of tax that chanced to be most convenient or acceptable to the public, were the general principles underlying the taxation system in North Carolina from the time of its formation as a colony in 1663 to the beginning of its separation from England in 1776.

Since the major taxes have been discussed in previous chapters, attention may now be given to the minor group. Among these casual levies may be considered taxes on land and on law-suits, and licenses. Lotteries may also be mentioned, for this method of raising revenue, though rare, was occasionally exercised in North Carolina.

The Land Tax. It was stated in the Chapter on Quit Rents that this feudal due from the land served to preclude the levy of a land tax in the colony during the colonial period. As a matter of fact, there was an exception to this custom during one brief period of the colony's history. In 1711 the Tuscarora War plunged the colony into debt, and the following year the state issued a total sum of £12,000 in "paper certificates of public indebtedness."[1] Two years later the amount of public bills of credit was doubled, in consequence of which the General Assembly, when it met in 1715, was looking for some new source from which to obtain revenue, having decided that it would raise two thousand pounds each year until its debt was paid. This body affirmed that, in addition to the poll tax, some other expedient for raising the sum of two thousand pounds annually towards paying the debts of the government was necessary. The decision reached was that a new rent-roll should be taken of the land, and that, with this list showing taxables and the number of their landholdings, a poll tax and a land tax should be levied upon the inhabitants with ability to pay them. In the paragraph of the act levying a poll tax of fifteen shillings per taxable, as the Chapter on the Poll Tax shows, was the following passage, expressing the conditions of the land tax: "That all and every person and persons in this Government holding lands either by Deed or Survey in their own right or as Guardians or Trustees for others shall pay the respective sum of two shillings and six penies for every Hundred acres of land as aforesaid."[2] In accordance with this law which remained in force for a period of five years, a uniform rate of two and one-half shillings in taxes was collected from the

[1] *Colonial Records,* Vol. II, Preface, p. iv.
[2] Clarke's *Laws of North Carolina,* Vol. 23, p. 91.

owners on every hundred acres of land in North Carolina from 1715 to 1720.

By 1720, however, the debt had been decreased to about half its original amount,[3] and the Assembly felt that it was time to reduce the previous heavy rate of taxation. It accordingly declared that, with the reduction of the poll to ten shillings, the land tax should be lessened to one shilling, eightpence, per hundred acres. This land always unpopular, apparently remained in force for only two years longer; at any rate, when a bill for revenue was passed in 1722, no land tax was mentioned.

As a matter of fact, there actually existed a tax on land for six or seven years in the colony of North Carolina; this tax, however, must not in any manner be confused with the land tax system which later developed in the province, after its Declaration of Independence from England. In the first place, this early land tax in North Carolina must not be thought of as a part of the taxation system; it was only an exceptional method of meeting a grave emergency. As soon as the special expenses resulting from the exigencies of the situation had been discharged, that particular method of taxation was abandoned. In the second place, this tax on land was not imposed according to the value of the land, but according to the number of acres. Here again, it was the number, and not the worth of the object, which was the basis of the tax. This idea of numbers seems to have been one of the distinguishing characteristics of the taxation system during the colonial era.

A Tax on Lawsuits. One peculiar kind of tax levied in North Carolina during the colonial period was a tax on lawsuits, which occurred a few times during the eighteenth century. In 1740 the state had appropriated

[3] *Colonial Records,* Vol. II, Preface, p. iv.

£12,000 sterling for bearing a share in the Spanish War,[4] and the colony was attempting to use all available means of taxing the inhabitants in its effort to lower the debt. In an effort to achieve this end, the judicial system having become firmly established in the colony, the General Assembly in 1743 passed the following law: "An Act to ascertain what Attornies' Fees shall be taxed and allowed, in any Suit of Action, brought in any of the Courts of Record in this Province."[5] The following excerpt gives the rates of the tax; "The several and respective Attornies' Fees hereinafter mentioned, shall be Taxed and allowed in the Courts following; that is to say, in the General Court, on any Action brought, or Suit commenced there or by petition, thirty shillings, Proclamation Money: in the County Courts, on any action brought or suit commenced there, or by petition, fifteen shillings, proclamation money."[6]

This tax on lawsuits proved so successful in raising revenue that in 1757, when the exigencies of war again demanded extra funds, in an Act "for granting further Aid to His Majesty for the Assistance of South Carolina and the Defense of the Frontiers of this Province, and other purposes," a tax on lawsuits was levied at the same time that the poll tax was imposed.[7] This was a tax of five shillings "more than the Clerk's, Sheriff's and Attorney's Fees" to be paid "by the party who shall be cast."[8] Lawsuits were again taxed in 1770 and a list was prepared regulating officers' fees in the province. This tax on lawsuits was an assessment or fee to be paid to the clerk at the time of issuing any writ, "or any other

---

[4] *Colonial Records,* Vol. IV, p. 421.

[5] Clarke's, *Laws of North Carolina,* Vol. 23, p. 213.

[6] *Ibid.,* Vol. 23, p. 213.

[7] *Ibid.,* Vol. 25, pp. 345–348.

[8] *Ibid.,* pp. 345–348.

leading process, by the Person sueing out the same, returnable to the Superior Court, the Sum of Twenty Shillings;
and if returnable to the Inferior Court, the Sum of Five
Shillings, for the Use of the Contingent Fund; to be re-
covered by the party cast, in the same manner as other
casts." [9]   This act was to continue for two years only,
but in 1773 it was reënacted, with the same tax on lawsuits attached.   This tax on lawsuits was one of the many
forerunners of the very successful system of licenses and
fees which later developed in the State of North Carolina.

License Taxes.   The system of licenses and fees in the
southern states has been productive of a considerable
amount of revenue.   This system, a part of the tax system
of the state today, developed from a few random fees and
licenses levied and collected, as occasion demanded, in
that territory during the colonial period.   So far as any
records indicate, the first act of this kind was passed in
1715, regulating "ordinary Keepers and Tippling
houses." [10]   Many years later, in 1741, we find that the
"Keepers of Ordinaries and Houses of Entertainment"
were required to obtain a license for running them, which
license should "continue in Force one year, and no longer;
for which Twenty Shillings" was to be "paid to the Governor or Commander in Chief for the Time being"; the
Clerk of the Court was to receive for "his own use," for
the license Order of Court and Bond, Five Shillings." [11]
This tax was again levied in 1767.

Other licenses were placed on various trades within the
province, and in 1752 there was passed "an act for licens-
ing Traders, Peddlers, and Petty Chapmen, and granting
to His Majesty an Impost or Duty on Goods, Wares, and

[9] Clarke's *Laws of North Carolina,* Vol. 23, p. 817.
[10] *Ibid.,* Vol. 23, pp. 79–89.
[11] *Ibid.,* Vol. 23, pp. 182–183.

Merchandise, to raise Supplies for defraying the necessary charges of Government." [12] This act placed these licenses at two shillings, eightpence, proclamation money for the Justices to receive, and twenty shillings for the Clerks to receive for the Governor, and for himself (the Clerk) five shillings.[13] This made the license amount to about twenty-seven shillings, eightpence. A similar act placing the license at forty shillings was passed in 1766.[14] Later, in 1770, an act which was to remain in force for two years, enumerated the list for placing licenses and fees and imposed the following licenses and fees throughout the colony:

11. Be it Enacted by the Governor, Council and Assembly, and by the Authority of the same, That for the future the following Fees only shall be received by the Clerks of the Superior and Inferior Courts; and no other or greater Fees or Charges whatsoever shall be Deemed or construed to be allowed by the former Acts of Assembly, to-wit,

For every Writ or leading Process returned to the First Court; and all subsequent Process, Appearances, Pleas, Rules, Orders, and other Services necessary thereon until the making up an Issue Inclusive; and also, for Dismission, or Final Judgment, where either Happens; or for concession of Judgment, to the Clerk of the Court, Fourteen Shillings.

For every Continuance, or Reference of every Cause after the second Court, including all Fees for every Service necessary thereon, Four Shillings.

For the Court at which the Cause is determined, including all Fees for every Necessary Service thereon, and entering final Judgment inclusive, Eighteen shillings.

For every Subpoena, more than three different and distinct Subpoenas, in any Cause, the Clerk shall be allowed, by the party praying such Subpoena, Two Shillings.

Provided always, that the Parties taking out any one of the Five Subpoenas intended by this act to be issued without fee may be at liberty to insert in each Subpoena any Number of Wit-

[12] Clarke's *Laws of North Carolina*, Vol. 23, pp. 371–375.
[13] *Ibid.,* Vol. 23, pp. 371–372.
[14] *Ibid.,* Vol. 25, pp. 498–499.

nesses, not exceeding Four, Two Shillings. When necessary for every execution or Order of Sale, issued and returned, including all services thereon, with taking Costs and Copy, and entering Satisfaction, Five Shillings.

For every Scire Facias against Bail, with making up an Issue thereon, or entering Judgment without Plea, including all Fees for every Necessary Service thereon; provided that the Party paying Costs, shall not be subject to this, unless the Scire Facias is requisite, and required by the Plaintiff, Eight Shillings.

For giving Copy of the Record of any Cause when demanded by either of the Parties, Six shillings.

For every Order or Rule of Court, made on Matters foreign to the Suits depending in Court, and Copy thereof when demanded, Two Shillings and Eight Pence.

For entering on the Minutes the Probate of a Will, Qualifying Executors, making Certificate, recording the Will, and giving Copy thereof, Ten Shillings and Eight Pence.

For granting Administration, taking Bond, and all other Services thereon, Ten Shillings and Eight Pence. For all services necessary to be done by the Clerk of the Court towards procuring Letters of Administration, or Letters Testamentary, if he furnishes the said Letters, including the Governor's, Secretary's, and private Secretary's Fees, Twenty-six shillings and eight pence.

For all Services in Proving, recording, and filing an Inventory, Accounts Sales, or Account Current exhibited by an Executor, Administrator, or Guardian or for Search Copy and Certificate of the same, if the Estate be under One Hundred Pounds, One Shilling and Four Pence; if above One Hundred Pounds value, Four Shillings.

For every Marriage License and Bond, and all the necessary Services thereon, Five Shillings.

For an Ordinary License and Bond, and all the Services necessary to be done, thereon, Five Shillings.

For Tavern Rates, Two Shillings and Six Pence.

For searching a Record out of Court, Eight Pence.

For proving or entering Acknowledgement of a Conveyance of Land, or other Estate, and certifying the same, with the Order for Registration, and examination of a Feme Covert without Commission, Two Shillings and Eight Pence.

For a Commission to take the Examination of a Feme Covert, or Witnesses in any Cause depending in the Superior Court, the Return thereon, entering, and all other services necessary thereon, Three Shillings.

For Guardian and other Bonds taken in Court, and for all

necessary Services thereon, every Fee relative thereto included, Eight Shillings.

For Indentures for binding out Apprentices, making Order thereon, and for filing and recording the same, including all Fees for every Service necessary, Five Shillings and Four Pence.

For a Special Venire Facias in an Action of Ejectment, or where the Bounds of Land shall come in Question, when the said Writ shall be issued, Eight Shillings. For a Special Verdict, Demurrer or Motion in Arrest of Judgment and Argument thereon, Four Shillings.

For Writ of Error or Appeal, with a Transcript of the Record, and all Services thereon, Ten Shillings.

For making out Certificates of Witnesses or Jurymen's Attendance, Eight Pence.

For recording a Mark or Brand, and granting Certificate thereon, if required, One Shilling and Four Pence.[15]

The licenses and fees imposed by this law, which was reënacted without any alteration in 1773, were not of any outstanding fiscal importance during the colonial period; their chief significance lies in the fact that in them lay the germ of the system of licenses and fees which later became so important in the fiscal system of the State of North Carolina.

Lotteries. No history dealing with the fiscal system of North Carolina during the colonial period would be complete without mention of the lotteries which were occasionally used in that colony for raising money. These instances were always local; no state lottery was ever allowed, although each local unit was compelled to obtain permission from the General Assembly for holding a lottery. Only three conspicuous references to lotteries are to be found in the laws during the colonial period in North Carolina. In 1759 "An Act for raising Money for finishing the Churches in the Parishes of St. James and St. Philip, in New Hanover County by Lottery,"[16] was

---

[15] Clarke's *Laws of North Carolina*, Vol. 23, pp. 815–816.
[16] *Ibid.*, Vol. 25, pp. 391–392.

granted by the Assembly. One year later that body passed "An Act for raising Money by a Lottery, towards finishing the Churches at Wilmington and Brunswick,"[17] and the following year "An Act to appoint Commissioners to further improve and amend the Navigation of New River, in Onslow County, to raise a Fund by Lottery, to defray the Expense thereof" [18] was passed. From these examples it is evident that the uses for which lotteries were permitted were varied. They were, however, always local charges, though the reason for their being thus limited in this colony is obscure.

[17] Clarke's *Laws of North Carolina*, Vol. 23, pp. 535–537.
[18] *Ibid.*, Vol. 23, pp. 542–544.

CHAPTER VI

LOCAL TAXES

AUTHORITY and Influence of the Local System.
In the South local governing bodies derived their authority from the central government, by which they were created and legalized, as agents for assisting that body in carrying out some of its laws. The local bodies in the South, unlike those of New England, were dependent for their powers and privileges upon the body which governed the entire colony. In New England, on the contrary, the colony was composed of an accumulation of several local bodies, each making its own laws and regulations. The colony of Massachusetts was representative of this type of local self-government in which the local body governed its own unit independently of any other power, and in which each precinct made and enforced its own laws. In North Carolina, however, as in the other southern states, local governmental conditions were the reverse of those in Massachusetts. There were at first no towns in the Province of Carolina, and a central government was established by England in collaboration with the settlers. The plantations were each managed and controlled independently by the owners of each estate respectively, each plantation having its own manor house which served as the nucleus for a self-sustaining, independent domestic economy. People did not settle in towns, as they did in Massachusetts, because agriculture, rather than industry, was the source from which the

southern people gained a livelihood. Since distances were considerable, communication was not easy and, to create a unified government, it was necessary to have some central body, which in North Carolina was always the source of authority. Gradually, when local bodies came into existence, they were originated and sanctioned by this supreme power and were consequently entirely dependent for existence upon the will of the General Assembly.

To a limited extent the local units in North Carolina were dependent upon the government for authority to levy taxes to meet their financial needs. Although the origin of the legal establishment of the colony does not antedate the beginning of local units by more than nine years,[1] the duties and privileges of these units were so restricted that local taxes, in comparison to central governmental levies, did not play any extensive rôle in the colony of Albemarle, which later developed into North Carolina. The Fundamental Constitutions, an elaborate and logical programme devised by John Locke and sent to North Carolina in 1669, proved to be of slight importance, because, although impeccable in theory, they were not adaptable to the practical life of the colonist. They were therefore set aside in 1691, and a practical government was gradually set up which developed out of the needs of the people. By 1729, when the Crown bought the colony from the Lords Proprietors, the nucleus of a permanent government in North Carolina was fixed. This embraced a local government with its precinct courts

---

[1] The Lords Proprietors were given this territory in 1663. The government was first established in Albemarle in 1664, by the "Appointment of William Drummond as Governor." Clarke, *Laws of North Carolina,* Vol. 25, Prefatory notes, p. 1. Eight years later, in 1672, the precincts of Chowan, Currituck, Pasquotank, and Perquimans were established from the "County of Albemarle." Corbitt, D. L., *Handbook of County Records Deposited with North Carolina Historical Commission.*

and precinct officers.[2] The expenses for the officers of the county courts, whenever they met, were, however, negligible, as their services were usually granted without recompense.

Until 1722 there were no courthouses in the few precincts which then existed.[3] This was about the time of Governor Eden's long, peaceful administration, during which the debt incurred as a result of the Tuscarora War, ten years previously, had been reduced to half its original size. In that year the General Assembly, which met in Edenton in October, passed an Act "for settling the precinct Courts and Courthouses."[4] The first article of this act explains conditions prior to that time: "Whereas through the great Taxes and Charges this Government hath laboured under, by Means of the late Indian War, there has been no Care taken by preceding Assemblies to settle the several Precinct Courts to any fixed or Certain Place, but have always hitherto been kept and held at private Houses, where they have been, and are liable to be removed, at the Pleasure of the person or persons owning such Houses, to the Great Annoyance of the Magistrates and people: For the prevention of which for the future" the act for buying one acre of land in each precinct and building a hourthouse on each lot was

---

[2] The machinery of the local government was composed of precinct courts and precinct officers who were the sheriff, the clerk, the registrar, and the coroner. In 1738 when the precincts were broadened into counties, Justices of Peace presided over these courts. Clarke, *Laws of North Carolina*, Vol. 23, pp. 122–127.

[3] In addition to the precincts established in Albemarle County in 1672, as mentioned above, five additional counties or precincts had been added: Beaufort and Hyde in 1705, Craven in 1712, and Bertie and Carteret in 1722. Corbitt, D. L., *Handbook of County Records Deposited with North Carolina Historical Commission.*

[4] Clarke's *Laws of North Carolina*, Vol. 23, p. 100.

passed.[5] For purchasing such lands and erecting a building on each, the Justices were given the power to lay "a poll tax on the several Inhabitants of their respective precincts, . . . not exceeding the sum of five shillings per poll per Annum." [6] From this time on, as precincts came into existence, there was a continual process—although often with lengthy intervals—of erecting courthouses and gaols in the precincts or counties. These expenses were generally met by a small poll tax on the inhabitants of the respective counties.

The routes over which people traveled to and from the courts were few and frequently hazardous, some of them on land, but the majority by water. The upkeep of the roads was not financed by taxes, as they were built and kept up by the physical labor of the inhabitants of the county. Each taxable person was required to work on the road for a certain number of days during the year, or to send a substitute in his place, a primitive custom which caused the maintenance of roads in the counties to involve no expense to the government. The presence of rivers made bridges and ferries necessary for facilitating communication, and the privilege of establishing and running ferries was usually granted by special acts of the General Assembly to individuals who were allowed to charge fees, designated by the legislature, for conveying traffic across the streams.[7] This was virtually a monopoly granted to the individual who established the ferry, but in this manner the public escaped the burden of paying

[5] Clarke's *Laws of North Carolina*, Vol. 23, pp. 100–101.

[6] *Ibid.*, Vol. 23, pp. 100–101.

[7] In December, 1754, the General Assembly made an exception to this rule by granting a tax not exceeding two shillings "upon the inhabitants of the counties for establishing a "Public Ferry from Newby's Point to Phelps Point," near the courthouse, on Perquiman's River. Clarke's *Laws of North Carolina*, Vol. 25, pp. 311–312.

taxes for this necessity; the upkeep of bridges, however, was one expense for which the local government was assessed. The establishment of new counties and mainte- nance of boundary lines usually proved to be one of its chief expenses.

There were no public schools in North Carolina during the colonial period. After the middle of the eighteenth century, when the colony had become prosperous, the leg- islature appropriated £6,000 for establishing a school, but this money was used for defraying war expenses, so that not a single public school was erected in North Caro- lina during this period. No local expense, therefore, was created in this field. The local governments also escaped expense in connection with the few tobacco warehouses which were erected for storing tobacco, the chief stable commodity used as a medium of exchange by the colonists, as the central government usually paid the expense of erecting and maintaining these warehouses. The care of the poor, however, was entrusted to the parishes.

Mention might be made at this point of the odd prac- tice of bestowing bounties upon certain phases of industry. Manufacturing was encouraged in a small way by allow- ing bounties to be paid for a partial maintenance of cer- tain industries which were deemed advantageous to the welfare of the colony, such as wool and flax, a custom which seems to have come into fashion about the middle of the eighteenth century. There was also the pay- ment of bounties for catching and killing wolves, crows, and pests of this type which infested the colony. These laws were usually designated under some such title as "An Act for destroying Vermin in the Province." The pay- ment of this latter type of bounties, which was usually placed upon the vestry and church wardens in the locali- ties, never amounted to any important fiscal burden.

The usual method of meeting local expenditures was through the poll tax levy upon the taxables of each county. While there seems to have been no general levy, from year to year county taxes were imposed according to the same principle as those of the colony in general. Whenever any special need arose, a tax was levied to meet that particular need; the rate of the poll tax in the counties, when not fixed exactly by the legislature, was accordingly fixed by the justices of the county courts. In the towns it was levied by the commissioners, while in the church it was placed by the church wardens. The basis for the assessment of these taxes was the list of tithables which was made by the General Assembly. Each sheriff was held responsible for the collection of the local and the general levy of taxes in his county, although the general levy always had precedence over the local levy. If a certain tax was imposed to meet some general expense of the colony and another tax imposed to meet some levy in a certain county, the tax for the former had to be paid, even at the expense of the latter, should the occasion demand. Each sheriff, then, was responsible for the collection and payment of the amount apportioned to his county in the general levy, as well as for the specific levy for that particular county.

At this point it may be opportune to examine the types of local bodies which had the power of levying taxes. These bodies may be classified under two distinct headings; under the first was that group of men concerned with civil affairs, while under the other were the men interested in religious affairs. Between state and church, therefore, a line of demarcation may be drawn for the purpose of studying local fiscal history in colonial North Carolina. The county courts and the parish vestries represented those two divisions; yet both of these bodies obtained their powers from the central government.

The civil effects of local taxation may now be reviewed. The expenses connected with the establishment and maintenance of counties and towns embraced practically all the expenditures for local civil purposes. Only Albemarle county was settled at the beginning of the colonial period in North Carolina, and there were no local divisions. Later, however, in 1672, this territory was divided into precincts and as the colony grew and more territory was needed, other precincts were established outside of Albemarle, until, by 1738, ten additional precincts [8] had sprung into existence around those of Albemarle. After the act concerning the building of a courthouse in each precinct was passed in 1722, a poll tax was levied on the inhabitants of each county to pay for the building of the courthouse and an occasional gaol. In March of the year 1738 the General Assembly passed an Act "for Altering the Names of the Precincts into Counties." [9] The fourteen precincts then in existence became counties, and twenty-one additional counties were organized from this time until the Declaration of Independence in 1776.[10] By the end of the colonial period there were some thirty-five

[8] These precincts were as follows: Beaufort and Hyde, 1705; Craven, 1712; Bertie and Carteret, 1722; New Hanover and Tyrrell, 1729 (Tyrrell was established from Albemarle); Bladen and Onslow, 1734; Edgecombe, 1735. Corbitt, D. L., *Handbook of County Records Deposited with North Carolina Historical Commission.*

[9] Clarke's *Laws of North Carolina,* Vol. 23, pp. 122–127.

[10] Northampton, 1741; Granville, Johnston, 1746; Anson, Duplin, 1749; Cumberland, Orange, Rowan, 1753; Dobbs (Dobbs was abolished 1791, and other counties founded from it), Halifax, 1758; Hertford, 1759; Pitt, 1760; Mecklenburg, 1762; Brunswick, Bute (Bute was abolished and Franklin and Warren were founded from it), 1768; Chatham, Guilford, Surry, Wake, 1770; Martin, 1774. Corbitt, D. L., *Handbook of County Records Deposited with North Carolina Historical Commission.*

counties in North Carolina, more than one-third of the number of counties existing in the state today.[11]

The commissioners for each of these counties were granted the power of levying a tax, not to exceed five shillings per poll, for defraying the expenses of the county; to meet the expense of building courthouses and gaols, each county as a rule levied a tax of a few pence or shillings, as the situation warranted, per poll per annum, for a period of about two years. In 1741 an act was passed in the General Assembly which stated "that the Justices in all and every County or Counties within this province, where there is not already suitable provision made, shall, and are hereby impowered and required, at the next succeeding Court of their respective Counties, after the Ratification of this Act, to lay a sufficient Levy upon the Inhabitants of the said Counties, not exceeding One shilling, Proclamation Money per Poll, for Two Years, for the building of a Court House, Prison and Stocks, or any such of them as shall be wanting: which Levy shall be paid and collected by the Sheriff of each County, in the same Manner as all other Public and Parish Taxes and levies are paid and collected, and by him shall be accounted for to the Justices of the County Court, upon Oath; and the said Sheriff shall be allowed Three per Cent. for collecting the same."[12] Not more than one shilling per poll could be levied for this purpose.

This rule appears not to have been strictly adhered to, for the General Assembly usually gave to each county, by special acts in each case, the right to levy upon the taxables of the county a certain amount for erecting a courthouse and other buildings. In April, 1743, the privilege of imposing a tax "not exceeding Two shillings and Six

---

[11] There are 100 counties in North Carolina at the present time.
[12] Clarke's *Laws of North Carolina*, Vol. 23, p. 181.

pence, proclamation money, for one year per Tithable,"
was granted to Bertie County, "for erecting a Court
House, Prison and Stocks." [13]   Another instance of this
kind occurred in 1748 when in April, the Assembly laid
a tax of two shillings for two years upon the inhabitants
of Granville County for "appointing Commissioners to
compleat and finish the Public Buildings already begun in
the said County." [14]   In January of 1764, the Assembly
levied a tax of two shillings per poll for two years upon
the inhabitants of Edgecombe for building "A Courthouse, Clerk's office, Prison and Stock" in the county.[15]
Later, in 1774, a tax of three shillings for two years was
levied on the taxables in the County of Bertie for "erecting a Court-house, Prison and Stocks" in the town of
Windsor.[16]   The general trend of tax levies for buildings
in the counties is illustrated by these cases.

When the building, inspection and maintenance of
warehouses was not superintended by the central government, it was entrusted to the care of the local units.   An
example of this occurred in 1740, when an act was passed
by the Assembly "to Enable the Justices of Tyrrell County
to build a warehouse on Scupernongs, for receiving his
Majesty's Quit-rents." [17]   Taxes were sometimes imposed
for purposes of this kind in the localities; for example,
that levied in "an Act for enlarging the Time for Inspection of Tobacco in the Public Warehouse in the Town of
Halifax; for increasing the Salaries of the inspectors of
the said Warehouse; for establishing Warehouses in the
County of Cumberland; and other purposes therein men-

[13] Clarke's *Laws of North Carolina,* Vol. 23, p. 215.
[14] *Ibid.,* Vol. 23, p. 285.
[15] *Ibid.,* Vol. 25, pp. 483–484.
[16] *Ibid.,* Vol. 23, pp. 958–959.
[17] *Ibid.,* Vol. 23, pp. 150–151.

tioned." [18] This act of 1760 contained the following passage giving the courts authority to levy this tax: "Be it
therefore Enacted, by the Authority aforesaid, That the
Inferior Court of Pleas and Quarter Sessions shall have
full Power and Authority, and they are hereby required
to lay a Poll Tax on every Taxable Person in the said
County, as well for paying and satisfying the Money
already due and owing for the Building of the new Warehouse aforesaid, as for erecting and building such other
necessary Houses as shall be by the said Justices thought
requisite, to answer the Purposes aforesaid; which said
Tax the Sheriff is hereby authorized and required to Collect, in the same manner as other Taxes are by law to
be Collected, and pay the same to the Court of their
order." [19]

The building of bridges also constituted a small item
of expense in the counties. To meet such an expense the
General Assembly passed an act to enable the Commissioners who should be named "to build a Bridge over
Livingston's Creek, between New Hanover and Bladen
Counties." [20] Not many bridges were built in the colony,
however, because ferries were at that time easier to
establish.

Another expense for which local taxes were levied was
connected with maintaining the boundary lines of new
counties. As new counties were continually being formed
during the colonial period, this charge brought considerable expense to the localities. In 1746, when Johnston
County was formed from Craven County, a tax not to
exceed two shillings, proclamation money, for two years
"and no longer" was granted by the legislature to be

[18] Clarke's *Laws of North Carolina*, Vol. 23, p. 512.
[19] *Ibid.*, Vol. 23, p. 513.
[20] *Ibid.*, Vol. 23, p. 151.

levied on the inhabitants of that area.[21]   In that year also
a tax of two shillings, proclamation money, was levied for
two years upon Edgecombe County "for erecting the
upper part thereof into a County and Parish by the name
of Granville County and St. John's Parish; and for appointing vestrymen for the said Parish." [22]   Again, in
1750, a tax not exceeding one shilling, was placed for
three years upon the inhabitants for defraying the expenses of the new County of Duplin, which had been
formed from New Hanover County.[23]   Precisely the
same terms were imposed in the tax applied that year to
the division of Bladen and Anson counties.[24]   Another
tax of fourpence, proclamation money, per taxable was
imposed in 1761 upon the inhabitants of the locality "for
adding part of Orange County of Johnston, and for ascer-
taining the Dividing Line between the said Counties." [25]
In 1764 a tax not exceeding one shilling, proclamation
money, for two years was granted "for erecting Part of
St. Philip's Parish, in New Hanover County, and the
lower part of Bladen County, into a separate county, by
the name of Brunswick County; and for dividing the
County of Granville, and erecting that part thereof called
St. John's Parish, into a separate and distinct County, by
the Name of Bute County." [26]   Upon the inhabitants of
Tryon County a poll tax of two shillings, for two years,
was imposed in 1768, for dividing it from Mecklenburg
County; [27] and in 1770, when Guilford County was formed
from Orange and Rowan counties, a tax of two shillings

[21] Clarke's *Laws of North Carolina,* Vol. 23, pp. 249–250.
[22] *Ibid.*
[23] *Ibid.,* Vol. 23, pp. 342–343.
[24] *Ibid.,* Vol. 23, pp. 343–344.
[25] *Ibid.,* Vol. 23, pp. 547–548.
[26] *Ibid.,* Vol. 23, pp. 622–627.
[27] *Ibid.,* Vol. 23, pp. 769–772.

for three years was levied on the inhabitants of Guilford. In that year, also, when Chatham County was made from Orange County, the inhabitants of Chatham were taxed two shillings per poll for three years "for erecting the same into a District County by the Name of Chatham County and St. Bartholomew Parish."[28] About this time, "An Act for dividing the northern part of Rowan County and erecting a new County and Parish by the Name of Surry County and St. Jude's Parish" necessitated the levy of a poll tax of two shillings, for three years, upon the inhabitants of the newly formed county.[29] The cases cited illustrate the usual rate of taxes levied per poll for the expenses of the local units.

Expenses incurred for maintaining the government of the municipalities constituted another charge upon the local units. The oldest town in the North Carolina colony, established on the coast in 1715, was "declared, confirmed and incorporated into a Township by the Name of Bath Town with all privileges and Immunities hereafter Exprest forever Pursuant to which it is hereby Enacted that Convenient places and proportions of Lands be laid out and preserved for a Church, a Town-House and a Market Place and that the rest of the Land which is not already laid out be forewith laid out into lotts of halfe an Acre each with Convenient streets and Passages by the said Trustees or any Two of them."[30] Ten years before, in 1705, this area had been incorporated into a township by the General Assembly which met at the "House of Capt. John Hecklefield the 8th day of March." Lots were usually sold at a nominal fee, and, after defraying the civil expenses, the remainder of the money was devoted

[28] Clarke's *Laws of North Carolina*, Vol. 23, pp. 827–831.
[29] *Ibid.*, Vol. 23, pp. 844–846.
[30] *Ibid.*, Vol. 23, p. 73.

to the use of the church. By 1724 the towns of Edenton, Newbern, and Beaufort had been incorporated; subsequently the following towns were incorporated during the colonial period in North Carolina: Woodstock, in 1738, in Hyde County;[31] Johnston, in 1741, in Onslow County;[32] Exeter, in 1754, in New Hanover County;[33] Halifax, in 1757, in Edgecombe County;[34] Tarboro, in 1760, in Edgecombe County;[35] Kingston, in 1762, in Dobbs County;[36] Campbellton, in 1762, in Cumberland County;[37] Windsor, in 1767, in Bertie County;[38] Charlotte, in 1768, in Mecklenburg County;[39] Winton, in 1768, in Hertford County.[40] In 1739, when the village of Newton was converted into the Town of Wilmington, a tax of five shillings was placed upon the inhabitants for two years for furnishing a court house, already erected, "and toward building a gaol in the said Town."[41] In 1746 the yearly tax was not to exceed one shilling, and sixpence per poll;[42] eight years later better regulations were instituted in this town, and the yearly poll tax was limited to two shillings per poll.[43] The town taxes were imposed principally for the purpose of building gaols and supporting the churches. The power to levy these taxes was granted in each instance for some specific use, and

[31] Clarke's *Laws of North Carolina,* Vol. 25, pp. 229–230.
[32] *Ibid.,* Vol. 23, pp. 170–171.
[33] *Ibid.,* Vol. 25, pp. 268–270.
[34] *Ibid.,* Vol. 25, pp. 354–355.
[35] *Ibid.,* Vol. 25, pp. 451–453.
[36] *Ibid.,* Vol. 25, pp. 468–470.
[37] *Ibid.,* Vol. 25, pp. 470–472.
[38] *Ibid.,* Vol. 23, pp. 755–756.
[39] *Ibid.,* Vol. 23, pp. 772–773.
[40] *Ibid.,* Vol. 23, pp. 773–775.
[41] *Ibid.,* Vol. 23, pp. 133–135.
[42] *Ibid.,* Vol. 23, pp. 234–237.
[43] *Ibid.,* Vol. 25, pp. 257–263.

in every case, the towns were compelled to receive from the General Assembly permission to levy their taxes.

In connection with town finances, it is not inappropriate, at this point, to speak of a curious tax which was levied on taxable males owning lots. There is a record of a tax levied on lots in the town of Edenton in 1740 and again in 1756. In the former year the General Assembly gave power to the town Commissioners or Trustees to "meet and lay a Tax on each and every Person, according to the Number of his or her Lot or Lots, Half Acre or Half Acres of Land, by him or them held within the said Town (Fronts excepted) sufficient to raise a Fence around the said Town, and Town Common, as the Commissioners or Trustees aforesaid, or any Three of them, shall think sufficient." [44] A penalty of two shillings, sixpence, in addition to this tax was imposed in case any one refused or neglected to pay. The Commissioners of this town were again granted power in 1756 to levy a tax "not exceeding five shillings for each Lot" upon the owner "to be applied towards fencing or ditching in the said Town," [45] with the same penalty for defaulting as prescribed in the earlier act. A similar tax was imposed in Newbern, in 1756, for building and maintaining a fence.[46] This type of tax seems to have been used frequently for the maintenance of the colonial town.

As a rule, the municipal charges were small and the revenue obtainable for their support was not large; the local bodies were, in consequence, financially unimportant. Although many small, so-called towns sprang up in North Carolina during the colonial period, the majority of them were no more developed than the average

[44] Clarke's *Laws of North Carolina,* Vol. 23, p. 138.
[45] *Ibid.,* Vol. 23, p. 466.
[46] *Ibid.,* Vol. 23, pp. 456–462.

cross-road settlement of today. The colony was chiefly composed of rural settlements widely scattered, and even though towns were being started, there was no noticeable development of them until many years later, after the colony became a state.

The Parish Levies. The second classification of local taxes lay within the jurisdiction of the church, the power to grant these levies being given by the General Assembly to the vestry. In some places there was a tithe, the so-called minister's tithe, which was regulated in the same manner. This parish levy was a local tax which was widespread and inescapable; the application of this levy, in fact, was so general that the Assembly regulated it just as it did the county levies.

"An Act for Establishing the Church and Appointing Select Vestries" is first found among colonial North Carolina records in 1715.[47] By this act the precincts or counties were sub-divided into two or more parishes, each of which had a vestry which consisted of the Minister of the Parish and twelve men whose names were mentioned by the General Assembly. The parish levy was always expended in the particular locality from which it was collected and was, therefore, essentially a local tax. These parish levies always took the form of a poll tax, to be used for supporting the clergy, caring for the poor, building churches, as well as for the purchase and upkeep of the glebe, or church, lands. In spite of this, a tax "not exceeding five shillings by the poll per Annum" was allowed to be imposed by the vestry upon the taxables of the parish.[48]

For the refusal or failure to pay whatever rate was levied, fines were imposed. Concerning these irregulari-

---

[47] Clarke's *Laws of North Carolina,* Vol. 23, pp. 6–10.
[48] *Ibid.,* Vol. 23, p. 10.

ties, the following passage from an act in 1720 "for Establishing the Church and Appointing Select Vestrys" states the law on the subject which prevailed during that era: "Where any Distress, Fines or Forfeitures shall become due by means of the afores'd Act that the Church Wardens in each and every of their respective parishes and precincts within this Governm't have full power and Authority (either by himself or Warr't under his or their Hand, directed to the Constable or some other proper person), to levy and make Distress on the Estates of all and every Person within their Several Limits and Districts for all such Failures, Fines and Forfeitures as by the Said Vestry Act shall become due, and the Same to dispose of as in and by the Said Act is provided, anything Contained in the Said Act to the contrary in any wise notwithstanding." [49]

As time passed and other counties were established new parishes were formed, some from the new counties and some from the old. An instance of this occurred in 1727 with the passage of "An Act to appoint the North West Part of Bertie Precinct a distinct Parish, by the Name of the North-West Parish of Bertie Precinct, and for appointing Vestrymen for the said Parish; and to appoint Commissioners in every Parish in this Government, to Call the Church Wardens and Vestry to Account for the Parish Money by them received." [50] There was another act passed about this time "for Regulating Vestries in this Government, and for the better inspecting the Vestrymen and Church Wardens' Accounts of each and every Parish in this Government." [51] With the advance of the

---

[49] Clarke's *Laws of North Carolina*, Vol. 25, p. 168.
[50] *Ibid.*, Vol. 25, p. 210.
[51] *Ibid.*, Vol. 23, p. 116.

century more interest was devoted to this aspect of local government.

"An act to enable the Commissioners hereinafter to erect and finish a Church in New Bern, in Craven County and Parish, in the Province aforesaid, and for the better Regulating the said Town; and other Purposes therein mentioned," [52] was passed, in 1740. This act contained the following provisions usually attendant upon vestry tax levies: "That a Tax of One Shilling and Six Pence, Proclamation Money, for Two Years, next ensuing the Ratification of this Act, be laid, and it is hereby laid on each and every Tithable Person within the said Parish of Craven, to defray the Expence and Charge of: building and completeing the said church, to be paid Yearly, in such Commodities as are hereafter rated, vis. pork, good and merchantable, dry salted, per Barrel, Thirty Shillings Proclamation Money; Beef, dry salted, per Barrel, good and merchantable, Twenty Shillings; drest Deer Skins, Two Shillings and Six Pence per Pound; Rice, per hundred, Ten Shillings; to be paid at such Times and Places as are directed for the Receipt of His Majesty's Quit-Rents, in and by an Act intituled an Act for providing his Majesty a Rent-Roll, for securing his Majesty's Quit-Rents, for the Remission of Arrears of Quit-Rents, and for quieting the Inhabitants in their Possessions, which said Tax shall be collected Annually and received by John Bryan, Gentleman, the first giving Security, in the Sum of Four Hundred Pounds, Proclamation Money, to the Justices of the County Court of Craven, for the Faithful Discharge and Payment of the same, who shall be allowed Four per Cent. for attending, receiving and paying thereof; and that upon Receipt of any Commodity or

---

[52] Clarke's *Laws of North Carolina*, Vol. 23, pp. 141-143.

Commodities, Sum or Sums of Money, for the Use aforesaid, the same shall be by him paid to the Commissioners,
or the Majority of the, or their Order, for the Use aforesaid." [53]   During the same year a tax was levied for a
similar purpose, namely, to finish the church in Edenton,[54]
and another in Wilmington "to the Church of the Parish
of St. James, to be built in the said Town." [55]   A petition
for using a "tax of Fifteen Shillings per Poll, on each
Tythable," for building the church at Newbern was presented in 1741.[56]

Throughout the colonial period, as the occasion demanded, taxes, usually of a few shillings, were levied in
the parishes, including a poor rate whcih was levied from
time to time.   An example of this is found in 1771, when
a tax of sixpence, for one year, was granted by the General Assembly to enable the Freeholders of the Parish of
St. John, in the County of Pasquotank, to elect a Vestry
and Provide for the poor.

The tithe for paying the minister's salary, the parish
levies for defraying the expenses of the church, and the
poor rates were all abolished at the close of the colonial
period.   When North Carolina declared its independence,
church and state were completely separated; the local
taxes for the church were no longer allowed by the government after the colonial period, and all taxes upon the
localities became strictly political.

[53] Clarke's *Laws of North Carolina,* Vol. 23, p. 141.
[54] *Ibid.,* Vol. 23, pp. 143–145.
[55] *Ibid.,* Vol. 23, pp. 146–149.
[56] *Ibid.,* Vol. 23, p. 182.

CHAPTER VII

CONCLUSION

A SURVEY of the taxes in North Carolina during
the colonial era is justified by the illumination
which it may cast upon the solution of economic and
social problems, since "fiscal conditions are always an
outcome of economic relations." [1] In order to understand
many of the peculiarities and intricacies permeating the
present taxation system of the United States, it is necessary to seek the facts of their origin and development in
the simple taxes of colonial times. Fiscal conditions in the
colony of North Carolina serve to show the extent of the
influence which English institutions exerted in the formation of this nation.

In analyses of the primitive types of taxation ingrafted
into the political and economic structures of the English
colonies distributed along the Atlantic coast in America,
the raison d'être of many constituents in the modern
systems of taxation existing in the several states of the
union is revealed. The majority of the rudimentary taxes
found in the colonies may be traced backward a step further to their genesis in English financial conditions. From
England fashions in taxation were brought over to the
colony of North Carolina. The transplanting of those
institutions from a so-thought highly developed country
to a barbarous and uncultivated territory, resulted in many

[1] Seligman, E. R. A., *Essays in Taxation*, p. 1.

alterations of them by their new environment. The modification and amalgamation of those theories and methods of taxation, in the region now known as North Carolina, participated in the forming of a unit in the general foundation upon which rest the modern forms of taxation in the United States. While North Carolina accepted certain phases of the tax system of England during the colonial period, she rejected others which were not needed. Other colonies along the Atlantic coast, having different needs, assimilated different forms of the English financial system. In a few respects North Carolina resembled her southern neighbors and her northern fellow-colonies in tax matters, but in many of them she differed radically.

When compared to that of other southern colonies, the political and economic organization of North Carolina shows many differences, although, generally speaking, her financial system rested upon the same type of social foundation. Virginia, for instance, was controlled by private corporations which operated for immediate commercial return; eventually, this organization was transferred to public control. North Carolina was owned by a group of English noblemen who interested themselves in making it a prosperous territory with the hope of future financial returns. Owing to inefficient management, however, this hope was never realized, with the result that the Lords Proprietors sold the land to the Crown. Virginia and North Carolina were also subjected to the same laws, imposed by England, regulating customs duties. North Carolina, in addition to these customs, levied duties of her own accord, for supplementing the payment of some of her governmental expenses. Her exports of tobacco, however, were not so pronounced as those of Virginia. Then, too, her citizens were more skillful in evading these duties. Consequently, the revenue from customs in North Carolina was not important in internal finances, while in Virginia, opposite conditions prevailed. In North Carolina, as in Virginia, the soil was fertile and rich, and the climate was mild; but North Carolina's coast was difficult of access, while that of Virginia was supplied with good harbors. The inaccessibility of her coast made customs duties in North Carolina play a less important part in the finances of the colony than they did in Virginia. All colonial imports, of course, were subject to certain restrictions which applied to all sections of the country. These restrictions caused the colonies to resort to other methods for financing internal affairs. The general characteristics of the taxation system in colonial North Carolina resembled those of Virginia; both colonies had their quitrents, their customs duties, their poll taxes, and their local taxes as the chief divisions of their systems. The principal difference, however, lay in the emphasis placed upon these various sources for obtaining revenue. In North Carolina the poll tax was chiefly used, in Virginia, the poll and customs, while in the northern colonies the property tax, founded upon an entirely different principle, was given the most prominent place in the tax systems.

Between North Carolina and the northern colonies, there was a decided difference in methods of financing affairs of government; their economic and social structures were different. North Carolina and her southern neighbors were agricultural communities, while Massachusetts and the northern colonies were primarily manufacturing localities. In North Carolina, where agriculture was the chief industry, a rural population necessitated some sort of centralizing agency to direct affairs of state; accordingly the central government became strong. In Massachusetts and the northern colonies, however, where manufacturing was the most popular industry, people settled in small compact areas, each governing itself according to its particular needs. The government, then, comparatively speaking, was decentralized. In North Carolina and the southern colonies, financial affairs were centralized; all laws permitting the levy of general taxes were enacted by the central government. In cases where the local units desired certain levies for specific purposes, permission to impose these was required in legal enactments by the central powers in the colony. In the northern colonies, however, especially in Massachusetts, financial matters were decentralized and the prerogative for levying taxes was exercised by the local units. The cause for this fundamental distinction in the methods of levying taxes in these two sections of the country, is to be found in the differences in the political organizations, which, in turn, rested upon unlike social and economic constructions.

The most outstanding dissimilarity between the systems of taxation in use in colonial North Carolina and those in the northern colonies centered around the property tax. In North Carolina there was no property tax, while in the northern colonies that type of tax formed the basis of the system. During the seventeenth century, the property tax was used in the northern colonies to finance special undertakings, but later it became a fixed source of revenue. In North Carolina and in most of the southern colonies, on the other hand, the poll tax together with the export duties on tobacco in some states was sufficient for meeting expenses; above all, quit-rents on the land were primarily responsible for the absence of a land tax in this section. Customs duties never produced any great amount of revenue in this colony. The poll tax, an expedient of primitive societies, therefore, formed the chief source of revenue in North Carolina.

The ultimate reason for the basic difference between the two types of systems, exemplified in the theories underlying each fiscal system, sprang from the economic and social foundation. In the North, where wealth was quite evenly diffused among the inhabitants, where no slaves existed, since each man was of equal social status with his neighbor, there was no concentration of wealth in one class such as appeared in the South. The individuals in the North, through their own labor, were the wealth getters. Consequently, property in an inanimate form—not slaves, with productive ability—was considered the source from which to gather taxes. As a result of this condition, an earnings tax [2] was appended to the property tax. There, the measure of ability to pay was based upon possession; this took the form of the general property tax. Casting a glance southward, where slaves abounded, the poll tax was found to measure ability in conformity to the capacity for production. Natural agents, such as land and all types of real estate, were regarded as elements essential to production, but as inactive and unproductive without the motivating force of human labor. The wealth thus created would be proportionate to the amount of labor expended in its production. A tax, therefore, laid upon labor would fall upon the source of wealth and form an adequate measure for gauging the proportion of wealth to be deducted for fiscal purposes. In other words, since labor produced wealth, the incidence of the tax would devolve upon labor. A poll

[2] Professor Seligman suggested the term *earnings* or *produce* to designate this type of tax. Since these "faculty taxes were not income taxes at all," but were "simply an addendum to the early land taxes, originally levied on product . . . to claim, then, that our colonial taxes on faculty were income taxes, betrays a confusion of thought and an ignorance of economic distinctions" (*The Income Tax,* pp. 386–387; see also *Essays in Taxation,* p. 19).

tax, then, upon capital and labor—which were combined in the possession of one person in a society where slavery existed—would rest at the same time upon accumulated wealth and upon power for producing exchange value. Consequently, earnings and property in North Carolina could not be separated, for the slaves represented a fusion of both. As a result of their economic philosophy, therefore, the fundamental principle of taxation in North Carolina was based upon productivity, as contrasted to that of the northern states, which was based upon property.

But why did this difference exist between the southern and northern colonies? The majority of the inhabitants in both types of colonies migrated from the same country, spoke the same language, held the same ideals, and in their new domiciles were exposed to the operations of the same political laws imposed by the Mother Country. What condition, then, in the new environment caused a divergence in the development of fiscal institutions? Was it not due to physical characteristics of the natural agents? The climate of one section was warm and temperate, while that of the other was cold and severe. In North Carolina, where the atmospheric conditions remained relatively constant and the average weather disposition continued moderate, the soil was rich in productive possibilities. In the North, where climatic conditions passed through many radical changes during the year, the soil could not be relied upon to produce regularly or efficiently.

In a rudimentary stage of society, like that of the American colonies, the type of soil in a locality largely determines the kind of wealth produced. The requisites for existence in such a community are limited to necessaries "for without necessaries it is impossible to live." [3] Con-

[3] Aristotle, *Politics.*

veniences and luxuries evolve gradually. In the South, since the climate was mild and the soil fertile, agriculture was the chief industry. In New England and the North, where the climate was cold and the soil not so fertile, agriculture was not carried on so extensively; there the chief activity was confined to manufacture and commerce. These forms of production led to the adoption of certain institutions peculiar to each type of social organization and necessary for its maintenance. Thus, climate affected soil, soil affected production, and the different types of production necessitated certain institutions which would aid in making each method of production most effective.

The chief difference between the institutions of the North and the South centered around slavery. Slaves were first imported to the country by the northern colonies for the purpose of their industrial advancement, but for various reasons, chief among which was the climatic conditions unfavorable to the existence of the African race, they proved unprofitable. They were then sent southward, where more favorable economic conditions caused them to flourish. "Thus," as Buckle would say, "we have man modifying nature, and nature modifying man; while out of this reciprocal modification all events must necessarily spring." [4] Fiscal conditions in the North and South, therefore, diverged, because they were based upon different social and economic foundations. Climate, soil, methods of production, resulting in certain institutions peculiar to each section of the country, were the underlying causes for this divergence. In this instance, environment seems to have played a major rôle in the shaping of early social institutions in the colonies. Fiscal institutions, evidenced in finance and taxation, reflect this difference.

[4] Buckle, H. T., *History of Civilization in England,* Chap. I.

The mutual connection between economic and political institutions is clearly shown by the establishment of slavery. Peculiar advantages and immunities naturally result in a society where slaves exist; social inequality is accentuated; and class privileges lead to social caste. Since it is to the interest of those who benefit by institutions to maintain those institutions intact as far as possible, the spirit of conservatism, generally predominating, is particularly noticeable in taxation and financial policies. This is the attitude which prevails in societies where the principles of aristocracy flourish, such principles always being based upon wealth and permanently fixed interests. Then, again, in addition to conservatism, this social disparity often leads to antagonism between the different ranks of people. This condition will be especially prominent in fiscal matters, for it is in that realm that the individuals in the community so often oppose their personal claims to the property prerogatives of the small number of people in the class with vested interests.

The result of an examination into the development and expansion of the primitive systems of taxation, may help, then, to render intelligible many of the obscurities which today surround the discussion concerning the organization of society with its complexity of institutions. "Institutions thus combine in the results of the contact of the mind of one society with that of another," and in so doing, they "are the organs that conserve what is best in the past of the human race, while to the individual they offer fields of ever widening activity." [5] It is, therefore, the light which the study of the original financial systems in the composition of the American commonwealth may shed upon the present-day social institutions of the nation which justifies this study.

[5] Giddings, F. H., *The Principles of Sociology*, p. 396.

BIBLIOGRAPHY

The History of Taxation in North Carolina During the Colonial Period, 1663-1776

ANDREWS, C. M., *The Colonial Background of The American Revolution*. Yale University Press, New Haven (1924).

—— *The Colonial Period*. Henry Holt and Company, New York; Williams and Norgate, London (1912).

ARISTOTLE, *Politics*. Jarrett, B. Translations of Clarendon Press, Oxford (1920).

ASHLEY, W. J., *English Economic History*. Longmans, Green and Company, London and New York (1892).

—— *The Economic Organization of England*. Longmans, Green and Company, London and New York (1914).

ASHE, S. A., *History of North Carolina*. 2 Vols. Charles L. Van Noppen, Greensboro, N. C. (1908).

Auditors' Reports of North Carolina, State Printers.

BARNETT, G. E., *Taxation in North Carolina*. The Johns Hopkins University Press, Baltimore, Md. (1900).

BASSETT, J. S., *Slavery and Servitude in The Colony of North Carolina*. The Johns Hopkins University Press, Baltimore, Md. (1896).

—— *The Constitutional Beginnings of North Carolina* (1663–1729). The Johns Hopkins University Press, Baltimore, Md. (1894).

—— *Landholding in Colonial North Carolina*. Trinity College Historical Society Papers. Series II, pp. 44–61. Durham, N. C. (1898).

—— *Slavery and Servitude in North Carolina*. Johns Hopkins University Press, Baltimore, Md. (1896).

BEER, G. L., *British Colonial Policy* (1754–1765). The Macmillan Company, New York (1907).

—— *The Commercial Policy of England Toward the American Colonies*. Columbia University Press, New York (1893).

—— *The Old Colonial System*. (1660–1754). 2 Vols. The Macmillan Company, New York (1912).

BLACKSTONE, SIR WILLIAM, *Commentaries on the Laws of England.* T. B. Wait & Company, Portland (1818).

BOND, B. W., *The Quit-Rent System in the American Colonies.* Yale University Press, New Haven; Humphrey Milford, London (1919).

BOUVIER'S *Law Dictionary*, Vol. I. West Publishing Company, St. Paul, Minn. (1915).

BOYD, JAMES, *Drums*, Charles Scribner's Sons, New York (1925).
—— W. K., *Some North Carolina Tracts of the Eighteenth Century.* Vol. III, no. 1, no. 2, no. 3. North Carolina Historical Commission, Raleigh, N. C. (1926).
—— and BROOKS, R. P., *Selected Bibliography and Syllabus of the History of the South.* McGregor, Athens, Ga. (1918).
—— *Currency and Banking in North Carolina—1790–1863.* Trinity College Historical Society Papers. Series 10. Durham, N. C. (1914).
—— *History of North Carolina—1783–1860.* Vol. II. Chicago, Ill. (1919).
—— *Table of North Carolina Taxes—1748–1770.* The North Carolina Historical Review. Vol. III, no. 3. The North Carolina Historical Commission, Raleigh, N. C., June (1926).

BRADLEY, H., *The Enclosures in England, an Economic Reconstruction.* New York, (1918).

BRICKELL, JOHN, *National History of North Carolina.* Carson, Dublin (1837).

BRUCE, P. A., *Economic History of Virginia in the Seventeenth Century.* Vol. II. Macmillan and Company, New York and London (1896).

BUCKLE, H. T., *History of Civilization in England.* Second edition. D. Appleton and Company, New York (1858–1861).

BULLOCK, C. J., *Essays in the Monetary System of the United States.* The Macmillan Company, New York (1900).

BURKE, E., *Speech on Conciliation with the Colonies.* Third edition. Printed for J. Dodsley, in Pall-Mall, London (1778).
—— *The Writings and Speeches of Edmund Burke.* 12 vols. Little, Brown and Co., Boston (1901).
—— *Works.* 16 vols. Printed for F. and C. Rivington (1803).

CANNAN, E., *The History of Local Rates in England.* Longmans, Green and Co., London, New York and Bombay (1896).

CHEYNEY, E. P., *A Short History of England.* Ginn and Company, Boston, New York (1904).

CLARK, WALTER (editor), *The State Records of North Carolina.* Vols. 11–26. Nash Brothers, Printers, Goldsboro, N. C. (1886–1907).
—— *Laws of North Carolina.* Vols. 23, 24, 25. Nash Brothers, Printers, Goldsboro, N. C. (1886–1907).

CONNOR, R. D. W., *History of North Carolina.* Vol. I. (1584–1783.) Chicago, Ill. (1919).
—— *Cornelius Harnett; An Essay in North Carolina History.* Raleigh, N. C. (1909).
—— *Ante-Bellum Builders of North Carolina.* North Carolina State Manual and Industrial College Historical Publications (1914).
—— *Revolutionary Leaders of North Carolina.* North Carolina State Manual and Industrial College Historical Publications. The College, Greensboro, N. C. (1916).
CORBITT, D. L., *Handbook of County Records Deposited with North Carolina Historical Commission.* Edwards, Raleigh, N. C. (1925).
CUNNINGHAM, WM., *Growth of English Industry and Commerce.* Cambridge University Press (1896–1903).
—— *Outlines of English Industrial History.* The Macmillan Company, New York (1896).
DEBOW, J. D. B., *Industrial Resources, etc., of the Southern and Western States.* 3 Vols. DeBow's Review, New Orleans (1853).
DOWELL, S., *A History of Taxation and Taxes in England.* 4 vols. Longmans, Green, and Company (1884).
ECKENRODE, H. J., *The Political History of Virginia During the Reconstruction.* The Johns Hopkins University Press, Baltimore, Md. (1904).
ELY, R. T. and FINLEY, J. H., *Taxation in American States and Cities.* Crowell, New York (1888).
FISKE, JOHN, *Old Virginia and Her Neighbors.* Houghton Mifflin Company, Boston (1900).
FITCH, W. E., *Some Neglected History of North Carolina.* Neale Publishing Company, New York and Boston (1895).
GIBBINS, H. DE B., *Industry in England.* Methuen and Company, 36 Essex Street, W. C., London (1896).
GIDDINGS, F. H., *Principles of Sociology.* The Macmillan Company. London and New York (1926).
GUESS, W. C., *County Government in Colonial North Carolina.* James Sprunt Historical Publications. Vol. II, no. 1. Chapel Hill, N. C. (1911).
HANEY, L. H., *History of Economic Thought.* The Macmillan Company, New York (1921).
HANKS, F. L., *History of North Carolina.* Vol. II. E. J. Hale and Son, Fayetteville, N. C. (1858).
HENING, W. W., *Virginia; Laws, Statutes.* Richmond, Va. (1819–23).
HUGHSON, S. C., *The Carolina Pirates and Colonial Commerce.* 1670–1740. Johns Hopkins University Studies in Historical and Political Science. 12th series, V, VI, VII. The Johns Hopkins University Press, Baltimore, Md. (1894).

IREDELL, JAMES (editor), *Laws of North Carolina.* Edenton, N. C. (1791).

James Sprunt Historical Publications. Vols. 1–17. Chapel Hill, N. C. (1900–1920).

JOHNSON, S., *Taxation No Tyranny.* Printed for T. Cadell, in the Strand, London (1775).

KAYE, P. L., *English Colonial Administration Under Lord Clarendon,* 1660–1667. Vol. 23. Johns Hopkins University Press, Baltimore, Md. (1905).

LAWSON, JOHN, *The History of Carolina, Containing the Exact Description and Natural History of that Country.* Strother & Marcom, Printers, Raleigh, N. C. (1860).

LINGLEY, C. R., *The Transition in Virginia from Colony to Commonwealth.* Columbia University Studies. Vol. 26. Longmans, Green and Company, New York (1910).

MARTIN, F. X., *Revisal of "Laws of North Carolina."* 2 Vols. Newbern, N. C. (1804).

MILLER, E. I., *The Legislature of the Province of Virginia, Its Integral Development.* Columbia University Studies. Vol. 28. The Macmillan Company, New York (1907).

MORGAN, L. N., *Land Tenure in Proprietary North Carolina.* James Sprunt Historical Publication. Vol. 12, no. 1. North Carolina Historical Society, Chapel Hill, N. C. (1912).

MOULTRIE, WM., *Memoirs of the American Revolution.* Longworth, New York (1802).

OLDMIXON, JOHN, *The British Empire in America.* 2 Vols. London (1708).

OSGOOD, H. L., *The American Colonies in the Eighteenth Century.* Columbia University Press, New York (1924).

—— *The American Colonies in the Seventeenth Century.* The Macmillan Company, New York and London (1904).

PALGRAVE, R. H. I., *Dictionary of Political Economy.* The Macmillan Company, New York and London (1894–1901).

PAULDING, J. K., *Letters from the South.* I. Eastburn and Company, New York (1817).

PEELE, W. J., *Lives of Distinguished North Carolinians.* North Carolina Publishing Society. Raleigh, N. C. (1898).

PROPER, E. E., *Colonial Immigration Laws.* Columbia University Studies. Vol. 12 (1899–1900).

Public Laws of North Carolina—1777–1926. Publishers vary; at present, Edward and Broughton, The State Printers, Raleigh, N. C.

RAPER, C. L., *North Carolina: A Study in English Colonial Government.* The Macmillan Company, New York (1904).

—— *North Carolina: A Royal Province—1729–1775.* University Press, Chapel Hill, N. C. (1901).

RIPLEY, W. Z., *The Financial History of Virginia.* Columbia College in History, Economics and Public Law. Vol. IV, no. 1, New York (1893).

Row-Fogo, J., *Local Taxation in England.* Macmillan and Company, Ltd., London; The Macmillan Company, New York (1912).

SANDERS, W. L. (editor), *The Colonial Records.* Vols. I-X. Nash Brothers, Printers, Goldsboro, N. C. (1886-1907).

SCHMOLLER, GUSTAV, *The Mercantile System and Its Historical Significance.* The Macmillan Company, New York (1896)

SELIGMAN, E. R. A., *Finance Statistics of the American Commonwealths.* American Statistical Association Publication, Boston (1889).

—— *The Income Tax.* The Macmillan Company, New York (1914).

—— *The Classification of Public Revenues.* Quarterly Journal of Economics. Vol. III. Boston (1893).

—— *The Taxation of Corporations.* Political Science Quarterly. Vol. V. New York (1890).

—— *The General Property Tax.* Political Science Quarterly. Vol. V. New York (1890).

—— *On the Shifting and Incidence of Taxation.* American Economic Association Publications, Baltimore, Md. (1892).

—— *Essays in Taxation.* The Macmillan Company, New York (1900).

SIKES, E. W., *The Transition of North Carolina from Colony to Commonwealth.* Johns Hopkins University Press, Baltimore, Md. (1898).

SIMKHOVITCH, V. G., *Toward the Understanding of Jesus and other Historical Studies.* The Macmillan Company, New York (1921).

SMYTH, J. F. D., *A Tour in the U. S. of America.* Vol. I. Printed for G. Robinson, J. Robson, and J. Sewell, London (1784).

SPRUNT, JONES, *Chronicles of the Cape Fear River.* Edwards and Broughton Printing Co., Raleigh, N. C. (1914).

SYDENSTRICKER, EDGAR, *A Brief History of Taxation in Virginia.* Bottom, Superintendent Public Printing, Richmond, Va. (1915).

Treasurers' Reports of North Carolina, State Printers.

Trinity College Historical Society Papers. Durham, N. C. (1877-1922)

VINOGRADOFF, P., *Villainage in England.* At the Clarendon Press, Oxford (1892).

WADDELL, A. M., *A Colonial Officer and His Times—1754-1773.* Raleigh, N. C. (1890).

WALKER, F. A., *The Basis of Taxation.* Political Science Quarterly. Vol. III. New York (1888).

—— S. R., *Memoirs of the Honorable Felix Walker of North Carolina.* A. Taylor, Printer, New Orleans, La. (1877).

WEAVER, C. C., *Internal Improvements in North Carolina Previous to 1860.* Johns Hopkins University Studies. Vol. XXI. Baltimore, Md. (1903).

WEBSTER'S *New International Dictionary.* G. and C. Merriam Company, Springfield, Mass. (1923).

WEEKS, S. B., *The Religious Development in the Province of North Carolina.* Johns Hopkins University Studies in Historical and Political Science. 10 Series. The Johns Hopkins Press, Baltimore, Md. (1892).

—— *The State Records of North Carolina.* Index to the Colonial and State Records of North Carolina. Vols. I–XXV. Goldsboro, N. C., and Raleigh, N. C. (1909–1914).

—— *Church and State in North Carolina.* Johns Hopkins University Studies. Vol. XI. Baltimore, Md. (1893).

WILLIAMSON, HUGH, *Letters of Sylvius,* essay on the Consequence of Emitting Paper Money. Trinity College Historical Society Papers. Series 11. Durham, N. C. (1915).

WOLCOTT, O., *Report (1796) on a Plan for Laying and Collecting Direct Taxes by Appointment Among the Commonwealths.* American State Papers, Finance. Vol. I. Washington (1832).

INDEX